GAMES
FAMILIES PLAY

GAMES
FAMILIES PLAY

GOD'S GAME PLAN
FOR A WINNING FAMILY

TODD HUDSON

Pleasant Word

Pleasant Word (a division of WinePress Publishing, PO Box 428, Enumclaw, WA 98022) functions only as book publisher. As such, the ultimate design, content, editorial accuracy, and views expressed or implied in this work are those of the author.

Unless otherwise noted, all Scriptures are taken from the Holy Bible, New International Version, Copyright © 1973, 1978, 1984 by the International Bible Society. Used by permission of Zondervan Publishing House. The "NIV" and "New International Version" trademarks are registered in the United States Patent and Trademark Office by International Bible Society.

Scripture references marked KJV are taken from the King James Version of the Bible.

Scripture references marked NASB are taken from the New American Standard Bible, © 1960, 1963, 1968, 1971, 1972, 1973, 1975, 1977 by The Lockman Foundation. Used by permission.

ISBN 1-4141-0420-0
Library of Congress Catalog Card Number: 2005901509

Table of Contents

Dedication

I dedicate this book to my wonderful wife, Tricia, and fantastic children, Michael, David, Joshua, Adam, and Rachel. Though we are far from a perfect family, I wouldn't want to participate in the Games Families Play with anyone else.

· ·

The Newlywed Game

Establishing a Lasting Foundation

As a pastor, I have had the privilege of participating in the union of many husbands and wives. The way it usually works is like this: a couple sets up an appointment, comes into my office, and asks me if I would be available on a certain date to marry them. They can hardly contain their excitement as they announce their intention to spend the rest of their lives together. Following that initial meeting, we spend time together in premarital counseling, preparing them for marriage, and they spend a large amount of time preparing for the wedding itself. Ultimately, it all climaxes with what typically is an elaborate wedding ceremony.

As I have counseled these ecstatic couples, I have never once heard anyone say, "We've decided to get married, and if it doesn't work out, it's no big deal. We'll move on to someone else until we find the right person." I've also never heard, "I have come to the conclusion that he/she isn't the right person for me. But I'm tired of being alone, so I'm getting married anyway." Now subconsciously, there may be people who think these kinds of thoughts, but no one would say this. Why? Because when we have made this life-altering choice to marry another person, we are already convinced in our mind that we are marrying Mr./Mrs. Right, and we are going to be one of the fortunate couples who will ride off into the sunset and live happily ever after. We all start out with these fairy-tale expectations that our marriage is made in heaven, so there is no way it can fail. But often what started out to be so promising doesn't always turn out that way, does it? While marriages may be made in heaven, they have to be lived out on earth. There are personality flaws to be faced, bills to be paid, dishes to be done, kids to be bathed and cared for. All of sudden, many couples end up readily admitting that what they have settled for is a far cry from what they had hoped for.

Susie was a typical four-year-old. She learned a new story at preschool, and she couldn't wait to tell her mother. So when her mom picked her up, she related her story almost in one sentence. "Mommy there was this boy named Prince Charming who had a white horse he liked to ride around and he saw this girl named Snow White lying on the ground and she wasn't moving and he stopped and he kissed her and she came back to life." Finally, after stopping for a second to catch her breath, little Susie asked, "Mommy, do you know what happened next?" Her mommy answered, "Oh yes! They rode off into the sunset and lived happily ever after." Susie frowned and said with a child-like innocence and wisdom beyond her years, "No, Mommy, they got married."

Many unsuspecting couples who thought theirs was undoubtedly going to be a fairy-tale marriage have ended up learning firsthand that getting married and living happily ever after are not necessarily synonymous with one another. How does this happen? Why do marriages that start out with such anticipation and excitement and enthusiasm sometimes turn into more of a nightmare than a dream? I believe it's because many have lost sight of the fact there are no fairy-tale marriages. No one rides off into the sunset and simply lives happily ever after. Every marriage has "for better and for worse times," and learning to navigate through those "for worse times" takes a lot of hard work, which will make or break a marriage.

My wife and I tied the knot when I was twenty-six and she was nineteen. When we met, it was love at first sight. The electricity flowed, and we quickly found ourselves caught up in a whirlwind, romance. We knew we were perfect for each other. We knew God had brought us together. We made the assumption that everything was going to be perfect, and we would automatically live happily ever after. But it was only a matter of weeks until we discovered, marital bliss was not going to be automatic or easy. There were issues that crept to the surface that had to be dealt with, maturity issues (not me, of course), extended family issues, independence issues (after all I had been single for over five years after college), and many other issues.

Whether you have been married for a few hours, a few days, a few weeks, a few months, a few years, or a few decades, you will also find there are issues that will rise to the surface of your relationship. It's your willingness to confront these difficult situations head on and deal with them that will make or break your relationship. Sometimes the challenges are unique to a particular marriage relationship, others however are quite common and faced by couples almost universally to one extent or another. What are some of these more ordinary challenges in relationships?

Unfulfilled Expectations

In my twenty years in ministry, I have had countless couples in my office who are struggling with their marriage relationship. Things aren't the way they thought they would be or think they should be. These couples' problems, while they may be stated a little different in each case, could be boiled down to one message, "We don't love each other the way that we used to." What they really mean is, "We don't feel the same way we used to feel."

Jack and Lisa were a typical couple who entered into marriage with intense romantic feelings for one another. They assumed those feelings would be just as intense every day for the rest of their lives. But when the routines and responsibilities of daily life set in, they found themselves with little time or energy left over for each other or their relationship. No longer did they feel the same intense romantic feelings and so by the time they came into my office they simply assumed they didn't love each other anymore and were planning a divorce. Their story is repeated over and over again in the lives of many married couples. When the newness of the relationship wears off and the intensity of their feelings subside, many people conclude they no longer love one another. Many couples want to give up on their marriages far too quickly and easily because they mistakenly equate love with romantic feelings.

It's no wonder we fall prey to this. Think about the language we use. We talk about falling in love as though we can't help it. It's almost as though we are saying, "I was walking down the street one day and I accidentally tripped and fell. I didn't see it coming. It just happened." And the implication is if we can fall in love with no responsibility, then we can fall out of love with no responsibility. Again, it's not our fault; it just happened. But what I want you to understand is that love is not simply a feeling. I guarantee you that as you make your way through year after year of married life, there will be times when you don't feel those romantic feelings for your mate with the same intensity that you felt them when you first fell in love. And if you equate love with those romantic feelings and the feelings are no longer as intense as they once were, then it's easy to think that you don't love each other any more, and you might as well get out of the marriage.

Remember the Percy Sledge song "When a Man Loves a Woman"? It's been on the soundtracks of several different movies. Have you ever really listened to that song? Think about the way it describes "falling in love." When a man is in love with a woman, the song tells us he can't keep his mind on anything else and he would be willing to trade everything he has in the world to hold on to this good thing that he has found. It even says that he would be willing to go so far as to sleep in the rain if that's what she wanted him to do! Now, come on! I've heard of sleeping in the doghouse but that at least offers some shelter. I think, undoubtedly, most men would be looking for plan B if their wife said, "I want you to sleep out in the rain?" I know I would! And he closes out the song talking about how much he loves this woman and will do anything to hold on to her love and then asks her to not treat him bad. You know what I think? She treated him bad when she told him to sleep in the rain! But these are the kinds of things we often think of when we think of falling in love. [1]

Do you remember the intense feelings you had for your mate when you first fell in love? I heard it said one time that romantic love is a necessary form of insanity. We wouldn't make a lifelong commitment to one person exclusively if we were not at least a little psychotic at the time. Even some of the phrases we use refer to the psychotic nature of romantic love. We say things like, "I'm crazy about him." "I'm madly in love with her."

While every relationship begins with those kinds of intense feelings, true love moves to levels that are much deeper than simply romantic feelings. My wife and I recently saw the movie The Notebook. It's an outstanding story of true love. A young couple, Allie and Noah, fall head over heels in love with one another in a summer romance. The feelings are breathtakingly intense, but her parents step in and separate the two because Noah doesn't have the kind of money or family background they desire for their daughter. They take her far away, hoping the two will never see each other again. Noah, pained over his separation from Allie, can't possibly think about moving on

[1] Illustration from "When a Man Loves a Woman" adapted from Bill Hybels, Demystifying Marriage, audiotape (Chicago: Seeds Tape Ministry, 1992)

to another romance. Every day for a year he writes and mails a letter to Allie. However, his heart is broken because she never responds. What he doesn't know is that Allie's mother has removed his letters from the mail and made her think he has never written.

After a year of getting no response, Noah finally gives up and tearfully moves on, as does she. He goes off to serve his country in war, thinking perhaps even the pain of war would be preferable to the pain he feels in his heart. Allie starts to date and finds a man suitable to her parents, and even though the feelings are not nearly as intense, she agrees to marry this young man and enter into the kind of life her parents have dreamed of her living. But Noah and Allie never forget one another. Finally, right before she is to be married to this other man, through a set of unusual circumstances, Allie and Noah end up getting back together and getting married.

The unique twist to this love story is that it is told through the perspective of an old man reading it to an old woman in a nursing home. You don't know it at first, but as the story unfolds, you realize the woman in the nursing home is Allie, and the man reading to her is Noah. She has dementia and can no longer remember who she is, let alone who her husband is, but he has moved into the nursing home to be with her and reads to her every day.

While that story may be fictional, it is repeated in the lives of people all the time but not always with the same ending. If a relationship is totally based on feelings, what happens to that relationship when sickness sets in and your mate can no longer even remember who you are? True love is more than feelings, but sometimes we get duped into thinking the feelings will always be as intense as they were when we first married. If they're not, we must move on.

Now please understand, there is nothing wrong with feelings. The Bible recognizes the feelings of romantic love as being legitimate. Do you realize there is a whole book of the Bible that is dedicated to romantic love? It's the Song of Solomon. Listen to what Solomon writes about his special feelings for his mate. "Like a lily among thorns is my darling among the maidens," (Song of Sol. 2:2). Isn't that sweet? My darling is like a flower among weeds. Listen to her response. "Like an apple tree among the trees of the forest is my lover among the young men. I delight to sit in his shade, and his fruit is sweet to my taste. He has taken me to the banquet hall, and his banner over me is love. Strengthen me with raisins, refresh me with apples, for I am faint with love," (Song of Sol. 2:3–5). Guys, I don't know about you, but that's the way my wife talks to me all the time! Romantic love is wonderful and powerful, but it's also very unstable. Feelings come and feelings go. The truth is it's a lot easier to fall into this kind of love than it is to stay in it. What happens when the intensity of these feelings subside? We may think we're no longer in love and we want to give up on the marriage. Remember Solomon, the one who wrote "my love is like a lily among the thorns"? Listen to what he wrote later. "A nagging wife is as annoying as the constant dripping on a rainy day," (Prov. 27:15 NLT). It sounds to me like he's speaking from personal experience and that the feelings are not what they once were. I am convinced that when many people get married, they are brainwashed by the whole idea of romantic love. Their expectations are that the feelings will never change, and when the feelings do change, they give up and want out.[2]

Uncontrolled Schedules

Remember when you first met how much time you had for each other, or should I say, how much time you made for each other? When we're young and in love, our feelings are so intense and the adrenaline flows so high, we can survive on little sleep, and we have a whole lot of energy to give to the relationship. I remember when my wife and I were first dating. We didn't want to leave each other's company,

---

[2] Rick Atchley, Why Marriages Need Remodeling, audiotape (Fort Worth: Rich-land HIlls Church of Christ).

so we would stay awake until we finally were ready to collapse and couldn't make it any longer. It would easily be one or two o'clock in the morning before we finally went to our own homes. We would be exhausted the next day, but we didn't care and even managed to stay up late again the next night because we simply wanted to be together. You know, I don't have that same energy anymore! I now find myself exhausted from the demands of my day and fall asleep in my easy chair at nine o'clock at night.

Isn't it true that when we are dating, we are at a point in our lives when our responsibilities are lowest and our energy level is highest? But then we get married, and the responsibilities dramatically increase. There are jobs to hold down, dishes to do, a lawn that needs mowed, a house that needs cleaned, diapers to change, kids to run to this practice or that practice, and on and on the list goes. If we use all of our energy sprinting through the demanding responsibilities of day to day living and don't have any energy left over to invest into our relationship, it's easy to find that after awhile we really don't know each other any more. Marriage requires investments of time and energy to keep the relationship strong. Many times we're so exhausted from life's other demands, we don't have the time and energy left to give to the relationship.

Unrecognized Flaws

We all know the story of Cinderella. She is beautiful and sweet and charming. The handsome prince is strong and hard working and sensitive to her needs. The two meet at the ball and the electricity flows. As the clock strikes midnight, she runs off into the dark of the night, leaving the prince behind, holding only the glass slipper that has fallen from her foot. He goes on a kingdom-wide search to find this woman who made an indelible first impression on him. He puts the slipper on foot after foot of young maidens throughout the kingdom, searching for the one whose foot fits. She is the one destined to be his princess. He finally finds young Cinderella. He marries her, and the story ends with them riding off into the sunset and living happily ever after. Deep inside we know that fairy-tale marriages don't really exist. Yet how many people when they begin to discover there are flaws that exist in their mate start to wonder, "Did I marry the wrong person?" When we asked our parents questions like, "How will I know whom I'm supposed to marry?" Or "How will I know Mr. or Mrs. Right when they come along?" Didn't we hear things back like, "Don't worry, you'll know." The message behind the words can be translated to mean that finding someone to marry is magical and mystical, and when you find the right one, you will simply live happily ever after. But the reality is there are no perfect marriages because there are no perfect people. Every person has flaws, and the discovery of those flaws can create a whole lot of tension.

Have you ever wondered what it would be like if they did a sequel to Cinderella? They could call it Cinderella Part 2: The Married Years. It would probably go something like this: Cinderella wakes up in the morning and sees how sloppy the prince has been—again. He's left his clothes all over the floor. She goes into the bathroom, and his stuff is scattered all across the counter, and the remains of his shaven beard cover the bottom of the sink. She looks and sees the toilet seat is up. She wonders to herself, "Oh, no! What have I done? I can't believe I'm supposed to spend the rest of my life with this slob!" She yells at him, "Why ain't you ever picking up after yourself no more?" He thinks to himself, "What have I done? Her grammar grates on my royal upbringing. I can't believe I've married someone who is so uneducated." He responds, "You mean, why don't I pick up my things anymore? Because I thought that was the maid's job, darling, and last time I checked you were well-qualified." The Cinderella sequel would be rated PG and suitable for families. I'm sure there would be some violence but definitely no sex or nudity![3] Cinderella

---

[3] Bob Russell, Myths about Marriage, audiotape (Louisville: The Living Word, 1990).

and Prince Charming could easily conclude, "I guess I married the wrong person!"

But every marriage is made up of two imperfect people. We all have flaws, and when we live up close and personal with someone else day in and day out, these are quickly revealed.

Sometimes we hear preachers refer to marriage as a divine institution. Have you ever really thought about what that means? Divine means designed by God. Institution, according to the dictionary, is a place for the care of those who are destitute, disabled, or mentally ill. If you put those two definitions together, you see that marriage is designed by God as a place to take care of two people with a whole lot of problems! What a great definition of marriage. No wonder good marriages don't just happen! A successful marriage takes a whole lot of hard work.

So as we face all these different challenges fighting against us, how can we have a marriage that lasts? How can we build a rock solid foundation that will conquer every challenge life brings our way and leave us with a marriage that survives for a lifetime?

The secret lies in the truth that marriage is a divine institution, which means it was designed by God. And when God designed marriage, He designed it for our happiness and not for our hurt. If we're going to have a marriage with a rock solid foundation that can survive the challenges of life, we have to build that marriage upon God's instructions given to us in the beginning. In Genesis, God established marriage, and the good news is He gave us some important instructions for a successful, lifelong marriage relationship.

When God created Adam and placed him in the Garden of Eden, he lived in a perfect environment—a spectacular garden. God also gave Adam a purpose for living. Adam walked in a daily, intimate relationship with God. It looked as though he had everything he needed, and he did—almost.

In the midst of this perfect place to live in and a perfect purpose to live for and a perfect relationship with God, the Bible also says that

God looked at Adam and said, there is something about this that is not good. It is not good for man to be alone. That's the first time we read that God ever looked at any of His creation and said it is not good. As you read through Genesis 1, it says that as God created the earth, sun, moon, stars, vegetation, animals, and everything else, He said, "It is good," or "It is very good." Now for the first time, God looks at his crowning creation, man, and says of Adam, "It is not good for man to be alone." Man's oldest problem is loneliness. What is God saying? Is He saying it's not good for man to ever be single? Of course not. The Bible teaches the exact opposite is true. Singleness can be a gift from God that allows a man or woman to really dedicate themselves completely to serving God. What God is saying is that He never intended for any of us to be lonely. One of the purposes for which God designed marriage is partnership. It helps prevent loneliness.

So when God recognized that Adam was lonely, God created a wife for him. He created Eve. Now let me take a quick sidestep for a moment and call something to your attention. Adam had a relationship with God that was perfect. He walked with God, and yet he was still lonely. At the risk of sounding like a heretic, I must point out that there are relational needs in your life that can not be met by God alone. You need an intimate relationship with another human being, and that's one of the reasons God established marriage. The opposite is also true. Your mate alone can not meet all of your relational needs. I have seen many marriages devastated because a husband or wife expects their spouse to meet all of their needs. No person can do that. There are needs in your life that can only be met by a relationship with God. We need both. You were created and placed here on this earth to have an intimate love relationship with God, and you desperately need that in your life. And you were also created with relational needs that can only be met as you walk in a close relationship with another human being. It doesn't have to be in marriage. But marriage is the most intimate of all relationships.

Let's get back to the story. Before God created Eve, He marched before Adam the elephants and hippopotamuses and zebras, and one by one Adam named them. I believe God did this by design. He wanted Adam to recognize there were two, male and female, of everything except for him. He helped Adam understand that there was something missing in his life. "So the LORD God caused the man to fall into a deep sleep; and while he was sleeping, he took one of the man's ribs and closed up the place with flesh. Then the Lord God made a woman from the rib he had taken out of the man, and he brought her to the man. The man said, 'This is now bone of my bones and flesh of my flesh; she shall be called "woman," for she was taken out of man'," (Gen. 2:21–23). When Adam first woke up from this deep sleep, this anesthesia that God had placed him under, and he saw Eve, what was his reaction? Well, as we read this section in the Bible, it is one of the classic reactions in all of Scripture. Can you picture the scene? Here's Adam waking up from this deep sleep. He's still kind of groggy. He's never seen a woman before, and he looks up and sees Eve standing before him. He rubs his eyes and tries to focus, and he thinks, I've never seen anything like this before! Now don't forget, he has spent the past several days naming the animals. He's been looking at elephants and hippos and zebras, and now he wakes up and standing there before him is this spectacular creation. God had created a gorgeous female from a rib in Adam's side, and she comes walking up to him with no clothes on! God asks Adam, "What do you think?" Now in verse 23 we read that Adam said, "This is now bone of my bones and flesh of my flesh." I think that loses something in the translation, don't you? This phrase in Hebrew is an exclamation, and literally, when Adam saw Eve for the first time, he said, "Wow! Far Out! Eureka! This is so much better than these animals I've been looking at! Whoa! Man! I think I'll call her woman!"

God Himself brought Adam and Eve together as husband and wife. Theirs truly was a marriage made in heaven. God gave them some basic instructions for living out this new, God-ordained relationship that are still important instructions for us today. It is the most clear and concise counseling session ever given for a successful marriage, and it was given by God Himself. It's a statement that is obviously very important because it's repeated four different times in the Bible. "For this reason a man will leave his father and mother and be united to his wife, and they will become one flesh. The man and his wife were both naked, and they felt no shame," (Gen. 2:24–25). In this verse, God gives us three building blocks to help us build a rock-solid foundation in our relationships.

Building Block No. 1: Leave

The first thing God says is that you have to leave your father and mother. Isn't this interesting? Adam and Eve didn't even have parents to leave. That makes it obvious that God was establishing a divine pattern that would lead to successful marriages for all time.

So God says first if you want to have a successful marriage, you have to be willing to leave behind your relationship with your parents. Does that mean you no longer have anything to do with mom and dad? Of course not. But your relationship with your mate has to take priority over your relationship with your parents.

I also believe God is not only saying to leave behind mom and dad, but He is establishing the priority of marriage over every other human relationship in our lives. He's saying this relationship is unique, and for it to succeed, it has to take precedence over all other human relationships. Notice I said, "It has to take precedence over all other human relationships." There is one relationship that must take priority over even your marriage relationship and that is your relationship with God. You were made to relate to God, and until you learn that and live that, every other relationship, including your marriage, will suffer. Marriage is not always easy. In fact, it can be downright difficult at times, and I don't know how marriages have any chance of surviving, let alone thriving amidst all the challenges that couples face today, if they have not started by first building that marriage on a relationship with God. That is priority number one. That is why you are here on this earth. The first and foremost purpose of your life is to understand how much God loves you and in turn wants you to love Him back. That's the foundation of life.

But outside of that relationship with God, you have to prioritize your relationship with your mate above every other relationship in your life. My kids are important to me. God has blessed me with five of them, and I love them more than words can possibly express; however, my wife is more important. Every human relationship in my life has to be secondary to that one.

When I talk about leaving your relationship with your parents behind, I'm talking about more than simply moving out of the house. I'm talking about cutting the emotional umbilical cord. Like a newborn baby can't survive outside of the womb of its mother unless you cut the umbilical cord, a marriage can't survive if you don't cut that emotional umbilical cord from your parents.

I see marriages all the time that suffer because this parental relationship has not been severed. I see couples where one spouse can't make a decision without asking mom and dad first. I see couples where every time there's a disagreement or fight, someone has to call their parents. I see couples who go home at every holiday and never stay at their own house or develop their own traditions. But if you are going to have a lasting marriage, you can't ask your mate to compete with your parents. You've got to make a commitment to put this relationship above every other one. This doesn't mean you can never talk to your parents again, but it does mean that your allegiance needs to change. Your allegiance now belongs to your mate. Your spouse should never have to compete with your parents.

Your spouse should not have to compete with other people either. While there is nothing wrong with having friends, your spouse should not have to compete with them for your attention. If every time your buddy calls, or every time your girlfriend calls, you drop everything to go do whatever they want, it will create an atmosphere of competition that will pull you and your spouse apart. Don't let friendships drive a wedge between you. Don't let your spouse get the impression that another friendship is more important to you than your friendship with them.

When you commit to someone as husband or wife, you make a commitment to prioritize this relationship over every other relationship in your life. If you are going to build a solid marriage foundation, it has to start with leaving.

Building Block No. 2: Cleave

The second thing God says needs to be present in your relationship in order to build a rock solid foundation is to cleave to one another. If you are going to build a successful, life-long marriage, you not only need to make a commitment to prioritize your relationship, you also must make a commitment to permanence. The idea of cleaving to your mate literally means to be stuck together like glue. It means to take two separate entities and cement them together. God is saying your union with your mate should be so strong that the challenges that could potentially pull you apart can't even touch your relationship because it has been cemented together with permanent glue—a permanence that you commit to on your wedding day.

My wife and I made a commitment from the time we were married that no matter what happened, divorce was not an option. We have never had an argument or disagreement where the idea of divorce was held over someone's head. That offers a whole lot of security in a relationship. If you want a marriage that lasts a lifetime, you need the security that comes from that kind of commitment. As long as we think, If things get tough, we'll get out, we probably will get out because things will always get tough.

When we said our marriage vows, we made them "for better or for worse." Please understand that every marriage has for worse times, and yours will be no exception. There will be times you won't "feel" romantic toward your mate. There will be times when you become so busy that fatigue sets in and your relationship will get pulled apart and you have to make a decision to slow down and once again, prioritize that relationship in the midst of a hectic life schedule. You will discover flaws in your mate that will drive you nuts, but God says if you want to have a lasting marriage in spite of all these things, you've got to be committed to permanence.

This gluing together that happens on your wedding day is the reason that divorce is so painful. Suppose you take two pieces of construction paper, one red and one blue, and you glue those pieces together. If you allow that glue to dry, those pieces of paper become cemented together in the same way a man and woman are cemented together in the bonds of marriage. What happens if you try to pull those papers apart? Is there a clean break? No. I have used this illustration many times, and it always works the same way. There's always some of the other color left on each sheet of paper. That's why separation and divorce are so painful. When you pull apart that which God has cemented together, each person leaves something of themselves behind. That's why God says, "I hate divorce." He's saying not only that He hates it as a matter of morality, but He hates what it does to people. It damages them. It damages families. It damages kids. So God says the best thing for you is to cleave. If you want to build a successful marriage, you have to make an unwavering commitment to permanence.

Building Block No. 3: Intimacy

The third thing that God says you need in order to build a solid foundation is intimacy. "The two will become one flesh." No healthy marriage can exist without intimacy. God intended for marriage to be a place where the two become one. Adam was one, but God reached into Adam's flesh and pulled out a part of him and made two where there was one. He then gave Eve to him in marriage and said now the two should become one flesh again. God established marriage to be the most intimate of all human relationships. Intimacy can exist without marriage, but no successful marriage can exist without intimacy.

The first thing that comes to our minds when we think about the two becoming one flesh is sexual intimacy, and that is an important part of it. God created sexual expression to bring intimacy and closeness in a way nothing else can. That's why God said it ought to be reserved for a marriage relationship. Any sex is a good thing because God created it to be a good thing; however, outside of marriage it is a good thing, in the wrong place. If you are not married and you're sexually active or living together, or you're married and having an affair on the side, you can easily be deceived into thinking it must be a good thing because that sexual expression still brings some of the good things God intended for it to bring within a marriage relationship. Things like intimacy, closeness, and passion. But here's the problem: it will eventually create a huge mess because it's in the wrong place. God designed sexual relations to take place only within the secure confines of marriage. It's the location, not the sexuality that's the problem. God placed boundaries on this gift of sex and said it should only happen in the confines of marriage because He knew what He had designed it for. It's a God-ordained means of communicating love, a mutually enjoyable means of sealing your commitment, and the ultimate expression of vulnerability and trust. When we understand that, it makes perfect sense why God would say that it should only be carried out within the boundaries of marriage where a lifelong commitment has been made. It's for our benefit that God says keep sex within the confines of marriage.

However, there is more to becoming one flesh than sexual relations. The kind of intimacy God is talking about here means becoming one flesh emotionally, spiritually, and physically. And that kind of complete intimacy takes a lot of work and commitment. In marriage, we face challenges that pull us apart if we don't work at our relationship. So God says work at your marriage. Become one flesh. Develop intimacy with your mate. (I'll give you some insights for developing this lasting intimacy in the next chapter.)

Notice with each of God's instructions, leaving, cleaving, and developing intimacy, I used another word—commitment. Each one of these things involves commitment. When we say "I do," it's a lifelong commitment. We make a vow to stay together "until death do us part." There is no escape clause in the marriage commitment. The problem with many marriages today is that many people who say, "I do," don't. Good marriages are a result of commitment, not convenience.

• •

Chapter 2

Love Connection
Developing Intimacy

A popular television game show in the 80s and early 90s was Love Connection. The show would have a guy, or gal, go on three different dates, and then they would come back to the set and tell the stories of their dates. With the help of the audience, they had to decide whether or not they had made a "Love Connection" with one of the three people. Isn't that what we are all looking for? Isn't that what we want in our marriages more than anything else? We want to make a "Love Connection." We want to connect with that person who is our soul mate, who causes our heart to race, and we want that connection to grow stronger and deeper over the course of time.

None of us are looking for a relationship where we simply find someone and then make a commitment to gut it out as husband and wife for the next fifty years. Yet, I talk to many couples who seem to be living precisely that way. They know they made a commitment, and they are willing to be faithful to that commitment, but they would also admit that what they have settled for is a far cry from what they had hoped for. If your marriage is a far cry from what you had hoped for, if you still find yourself lonely and at times craving a relationship far different from what you have, it could be because you haven't made a real love connection.

What we desire, what we crave, and what God created us to have is a real love connection that creates a lifetime bond of intimacy with our mate. While commitment is honorable and absolutely essential for a lasting marriage, you will be disappointed if you don't develop a level of intimacy where you learn to love your spouse and where you receive love from your spouse.

Notice I said, "Learn to love your spouse." We often talk about people falling in love and getting married, but what really happens in a successful marriage is that following that initial infatuation stage of marriage, we learn to love one another over the years. Adam and Eve were put together as husband and wife by God the first day they met. Granted, Adam could literally say, "Eve, you're the only girl in the world for me." But the reality was they had to learn to love each other; they didn't get married because they loved each other. Intimacy is something that happens over the course of time as two become one flesh; it's not something that happens automatically; it's something that takes hard work.

I relate to the illustration Willard Harley uses in his book His Needs, Her Needs of a Love Bank. He points out how each one of us, figuratively speaking, has a Love Bank, and we actually have a different "Love Bank Account" for each person we know. Every time we interact with people, they either make deposits or withdrawals in our Love Banks. Pleasurable interactions cause deposits, and painful interactions cause withdrawals. This is especially true in marriage. We have two different accounts: his and hers. Positive interactions, where love is communicated, deposits love units into the bank. Conversely, negative interactions deplete the account until eventually, if we are not careful, that account can end up bankrupt.[1] What kinds of positive

---

[1] Willard Harley, His Needs, Her Needs, 51st ed. (Grand Rapids: Baker Book House, 1986), 18–25.

investments do we need to make into the Love Bank of our mate to develop intimacy?

Time

We mentioned in the first chapter how one of the things that can pull us apart is busyness. Our schedules get out of control, and if we don't prioritize time for one another, we end up giving our spouse leftovers, our worst time, when we're tired and exhausted, if there is any time left to give at all. If we are going to make a love connection that lasts a lifetime, we have to make deposits of both quality and quantity time into our spouse's Love Bank. Sometimes I hear people say we may not get to spend as much time as we want together (quantity), but the time we do get is quality time. I don't believe if you have one without the other you will make the intimate love connection you are looking for. It takes both quantity of time and quality of time. If you spend a lot of time together, but it's spent sitting in front of the television or sitting in the same room but no real conversation takes place, it won't make a lasting difference. On the other hand, if you have some really good connecting time, but it doesn't happen often enough, the relationship can begin to fizzle.

You might read this and think, This isn't rocket science. This is really simple. Of course if we are going to connect with one another, it will take time. But in light of the schedules many of us keep, this can be easily overlooked. Many couples live lives that pull them apart so much that they become like married singles, two people who share the same house but never spend any real time connecting with one another.

Remember how much time and attention you gave to your mate when you were dating? You were totally absorbed with the other person, and you couldn't spend enough time together. One of the things I like to do is to people watch. It can be an absolutely fascinating thing to do. You can learn a whole lot about people from watching them. For instance, I have found that it's easy to tell whether a couple sitting in a restaurant is married or dating. If they are totally absorbed in one another, gazing into each others eyes, oblivious to what is going on around them, laughing and touching one another, my first thought is, Oh, they must be dating. But if I see a couple sitting there, looking bored, paying attention to everything else going on in the room, playing with their food, and there's very little conversation going on, I think, They must be married. That's definitely a bit of an exaggeration, but often it's more true than many of us want to admit. I don't believe God ever intended for marriage to be like that. He designed marriage for our help and not our hurt. He wants us to spend time together and enjoy the time we spend with our mate.

When a couple is dating, they usually have two primary goals in the time they spend together. They try to (1) get to know each other more thoroughly and (2) let each other know how much they care for each other. Let me ask you a question, why should these goals change after the wedding? The couple who desires a happy marriage will continue seeking to meet these two goals throughout their lifetime.[2]

For connection to take place, we desperately need time together. It doesn't have to be spent simply sitting and gazing into the other person's eyes for hours at a time, but it does mean that whatever it is that we do together we give our full attention to the other person. If you are sitting and having a conversation while trying to read the newspaper, you are not focused on your mate and connection will not take place. If you play golf together but are focused on the competition or the game more than each other, you have missed the point entirely. The focus of our attention has to be on one another to turn any quantity of time into quality time.

The biggest hindrance to investing time into the Love Bank of our mate is busyness. We become so busy with our competing schedules that often we don't make the time necessary to spend with one another

---

[2] Ibid.

to really fuel this love connection. What happens when we don't invest the necessary time in the ongoing development of our relationship? We naturally pull farther apart.

Randy Frazee, in his book Making Room for Life, writes, "Simply put, we have squeezed living out of life. We're always running around trying to get to our next event. This presents at least two major problems. First, our busy lifestyles create this toxic disease called crowded loneliness. But there's an even deeper problem. In our original design we were created with connection equipment. If this requirement is not met we will die."[3]

I believe he's right. Let me share with you a typical week's schedule at our household. I get up between 5:00 and 5:30 a.m. and do my quiet time and get ready. Some days, I work at home early in the morning and a couple of days I have meetings at 6:30 a.m. Our oldest son, Michael, has to catch the bus at 6:40, so he's the next one out of bed, although he is definitely not wired to be a morning person at this point in his life! About the time he leaves, my wife, Tricia, hits the snooze alarm for the second time and then rolls out of bed. She gets herself and our three younger children ready and heads out the door by 8:15. Our second oldest, David, dresses, eats breakfast, and catches the bus to school by 8:30. Tricia drops our three younger ones off at their school/preschool classes, and then she goes to the office and works all day, skipping lunch so she can get off early to pick the kids up at 3:30 p.m. On Monday night, I have an elder's meeting. Tricia takes David to basketball practice. Tuesday after school, Tricia drives David to piano practice. Wednesday, we come home, eat dinner, and rush back to Wednesday night programming at church. Thursday night is basketball practice for Joshua and baseball practice for Michael and David. At the same time, Tricia and I have a dinner to attend at the church. Friday is my day off, but there are

[3] Randy Frazee, Making Room for Life (Grand Rapids: Zondervan Publishing, 2003), 13.

errands to run, shopping to do, and chores around the house to be accomplished. Saturday morning I work for awhile to finalize my weekend message, then we attend Joshua's and David's basketball games and get home in time for me to go up to church and get ready for our Saturday night services. Sunday morning, of course, is church, and Sunday evening we take Michael to youth worship. In the midst of all this, there is homework to be done and laundry to be washed and kids to be bathed. Does this sound familiar? Our schedules so often pull us apart that there's no time for real connection.

We can convince ourselves that it's a stage of life that will pass and then we'll have more time to connect with one another. That may be true, but if in the midst of our present busyness we don't find time to invest in our marriage relationship, our lives can feel empty and alone, and we can easily be pulled apart. We must invest quantity and quality time into our relationship.

My wife and I try to combat this busyness by scheduling time alone together. We put it on our calendar and prioritize it. It is absolutely essential that husbands and wives schedule time to go out on dates alone. If you have not yet learned the importance of dating your mate, it's time to get started! Don't let courtship die. If more couples would court one another, a lot fewer marriages would end up in court! If you want to make a lasting love connection with your mate, take time for togetherness.

Talk

Another necessary deposit we need to make into the Love Bank of our spouse, in order to develop and maintain an intimate lifelong love connection, is communication. This is closely related to the first Love Bank deposit of time. We need to spend time together to communicate. Many couples today become so busy with their own things, that they don't really develop interests together. If we don't develop shared interests, our conversations will naturally be hindered.

Conversation is one of the ingredients we all know we need in a successful marriage, but I talk to many couples that struggle with how to do this. They sit in the same room together. They sit at the same table together. They lie in the same bed together. And yet, even though they are "together," they find themselves alone because, while there may be surface talk, no real communication, no real connection, takes place. Often this is because they live their lives separately, like married singles. According to one survey, the typical married couple in the U.S. spends four minutes a day in "meaningful conversation." That's 0.3 percent of the hours in a day. That's not enough time to really communicate is it?[4]

When we're dating, communication comes easily. We share our day with the other person, and they are totally focused on what we are saying, not because what we say is that interesting, but because they are totally consumed by who we are. We are the focal point of their attention. When you are dating and you are not together, you can't wait until you can talk on the phone for even a few moments. Remember how hard it was to hang up? "You hang up first." "No, you hang up first." No one wanted to be the one to end the conversation. I think most of us assumed that once we got married, the communication would come as naturally. But we quickly found that wasn't true.

Bill Hybels tells a true story of an older British couple he and his wife met while on vacation. This couple told about their wedding. They planned their reception on a cruise ship in the Caribbean. They wanted to create an unforgettable experience for themselves and their guests down to the last detail. The groom approached the head chef and told him he wanted two special items for the cruise: plenty of

---

[4] Illustration from Preaching Today.com submitted by Jeffrey Arthurs, from New Man Magazine (Jan/Feb 1995)

the finest champagne and mountains and mountains of prawns. The groom saw the strange look on the chef's face, and the chef asked, "Are you sure that's what you want?" The groom knew prawns could be very expensive, and so he told the chef, "Don't worry, I can afford it. I don't care how much it costs or what it takes to get them. That's what I want. I want mountains and mountains of prawns." So the big day arrived, and the couple and their friends boarded the ship for the reception. The champagne began to flow freely, and the groom was so excited, he couldn't contain himself. He took a couple of his buddies to the food serving area to peek at the white linen tablecloths, ice sculpture, and flowers. And sure enough, there they were: huge silver barrel-sized containers, concealing culinary delights! Wanting to show off, the groom said to his friends, "Look at what we're going to eat." He flipped open the lids to two of the containers, and there they were: prunes! Mountains and mountains of prunes! They flipped every lid, and that's all there was for dinner: prunes! Bill Hybels, who tells this story, says that at least the marriage got off to a running start, and the reception turned into a very moving experience![5]

If a wedding reception can be ruined because of one wrong vowel, how much more damage can be done in a marriage by choosing wrongs words when communicating with our mate? The way we talk to one another can have an extremely powerful impact upon our relationship. Words can make or break a marriage. Remember that little nursery rhyme we used to quote as kids, "Sticks and stones may break my bones, but words will never hurt me"? That's one of the dumbest things we ever learned to say because it is absolutely not true. You know from past experience that words can hurt you deeply. Some of you have been put down by a parent, torn apart by a sibling, or verbally abused by a spouse. You know that long after the words are gone, the wounds are still there and they hurt deeply. The Bible puts it this way, "The tongue has the power of life and death," (Prov.

---

[5] Bill Hybels, Demystifying Marriage, audiotape (Chicago, Seeds Tape Ministry)

18:21). The way we communicate with one another can either bring life or death to our marriages and our other relationships as well. So we have to work hard at it. Yet many of us struggle.

Why do most marriages, at least early on, struggle to some degree or another with communication? One reason is because we have different communication styles. We come from different backgrounds. And like it or not, for better or for worse, the communication style you learned in the family you grew up in is brought into your marriage. For instance, in the family I grew up in, we had no trouble expressing ourselves. Conversations were straightforward, expressive, and could occasionally get a little loud. My wife's family, on the other hand, was more quiet and reserved. They didn't express feelings as openly. We quickly found that this created some issues for us, and so she had to learn to adjust! (Okay, so did I!)

Your gender also has something to do with your communication style. In a Harvard study of several hundred preschoolers, researchers discovered an interesting phenomenon. As they taped the children's playground conversation, they realized that all the sounds coming from little girls' mouths were recognizable words. However, only 60 percent of the sounds coming from little boys were recognizable. The other 40 percent were yells and sound effects like "Vrrrooooom!" "Aaaaagh!" "Toot toot!" This difference persists into adulthood. Communication experts say that the average, woman speaks over twenty-five thousand words a day, while the average, man speaks only a little over ten thousand. What does this mean in marital terms? On average a wife will say she needs to spend forty-five minutes to an hour each day in meaningful conversation with her husband. What does her husband, sitting next to her, say is enough time for meaningful conversation? Fifteen to twenty minutes—once or twice a week! That is why, wives, when you ask your husband how his day was, he simply grunts and says fine, or awful, but doesn't want to expound upon it. He's already used up all his words before he came home! And, guys, that's why when you walk in the door, your wife wants to tell you every detail of her day. She's still got fifteen thousand words left!⁶

Several years ago, there was a popular book titled Men Are from Mars, Women Are from Venus. When you stop and think about it, that's true when it comes to conversation. We are from different planets! We speak different languages! When a woman talks to a man, he's often thinking, I'm waiting for the point. What information am I supposed to get from this conversation? But for the woman, the conversation itself is the point. She wants to converse. She wants to be heard. She wants to connect with her husband—not simply share information.

Can we get past this gender gap we have in communication and learn to communicate with one another effectively in such a way that our words bring life and not death? I believe so. I believe that communication is a skill that can be learned. The Bible offers tremendous insight into what effective communication looks like. An insightful passage for developing effective communication skills is James 1:19, "My dear brothers, take note of this: Everyone should be quick to listen, slow to speak and slow to become angry."

1. Effective communication begins with quick listening. James says, "Everyone should be quick to listen." Most of you are thinking, Why are you mentioning listening? This section is on talking. I don't want to know how I can hear better, I want to know how I can be heard better. Or you're thinking, Maybe this part will be good for my spouse because he/she never really listens to me. But all of us can learn to become more effective listeners. How can you say things that meet the needs of your mate effectively if you don't first listen to discern what those needs are?
    Chuck Swindoll, in his book Stress Fractures, tells of a time when he found himself with too many commitments in too few days. He

⁶ Rick Atchley, Making Room for Talk, audiotape (Fort Worth: Richland Hills Church of Christ).

got nervous and tense about it. He wrote, "I was snapping at my wife and our children, choking down my food at mealtimes, and feeling irritated at unexpected interruptions. Before long, things around our home started reflecting the pattern of my hurry-up style. It was becoming unbearable. I distinctly remember after supper one evening, the words of our younger daughter, Colleen. She wanted to tell me something important that had happened to her at school that day. She began hurriedly, 'Daddy, I wanna tell you somethin' and I'll tell you really fast.' Suddenly realizing her frustration, I answered, 'Honey, you can tell me—and you don't have to tell me really fast. Say it slowly.' "Swindoll said, "I'll never forget her answer: 'Then listen slowly'."[7]

We have to work at developing this skill of listening. Let me share a few suggestions that I think will help you develop the art of listening.

- Listen with your eyes focused. Look at your spouse when he/she is talking to you. There is something critical about eye contact when it comes to listening. When your eyes are focused on the other person, it shuts out distractions, and it communicates the message you are important and you have my full attention. Don't try to listen to your spouse while watching television, looking at the newspaper, reading a book, or doing anything else. Give them your complete attention.

- Listen with your mouth closed. I have heard it said that most people only listen for seventeen seconds before interjecting their own words. Let your spouse finish with their thoughts without being interrupted. Don't interrupt in your mind either. By that I mean, don't be thinking about your response. When you do, you can't hear what they are saying.

---

[7] Charles Swindoll, Stress Fractures (Portland, OR: Multnomah Press, 1990), 163–164.

- Listen for unspoken words. Pay attention to tone and body language. Those things may communicate feelings that never come across in the words themselves. This is important because body language and tone often communicate a great deal of important information. I hate to communicate about sensitive things by e-mail. I have found that when someone sends me an e-mail, I can't tell from the words if they are offering advice or if they are angry. Are they concerned or are they condemning? Make sure to pay attention to what the unspoken words are communicating. If we are going to communicate with one another, we can't do all the talking! We have to learn to be good listeners. Communication is a two-way street.

2. Effective communication involves choosing your words wisely. I think that's what James means with his second piece of advice—"Be slow to speak." Too often we speak too quickly and stick our foot in our mouth because we haven't taken time to think about what we are saying. I am a master at speaking too quickly. I tend to anticipate what Tricia is saying and respond before she even finishes her question or comment. Many times I end up looking foolish because I was anticipating something that she wasn't even saying. If we would slow down our speaking, it would help us in our listening and keep us from looking foolish. The Bible reminds us that we should, "Listen before you answer. If you don't, you are being stupid and insulting," (Prov. 18:13 TEV). When I am too quick to speak, that's exactly what happens. I look stupid or end up saying something insulting. Take time before you speak, and try to reflect on how those words are going to sound to your mate. We must be wise in the words we choose because words can build up or tear down, pull us together or pull us apart, inflame or defuse a conflict. Be slow to speak.

3. Effective communication means being slow to anger. Have you noticed that in many marriages there seems to be one who blows up and one who clams up? And many times the clamming up by the one spouse is a direct result of the blowing up of the other spouse. When someone gets angry and lets loose with harsh words, it hinders communication. That's why the Bible says in Ephesians 4:26 "In your anger do not sin: Do not let the sun go down while you are still angry." We are going to have anger in marriage. We will hurt each other. Our feelings will get wounded. But we have to learn to deal with it appropriately (in your anger do not sin) and immediately (do not let the sun go down).

It reminds me of a story I heard about a little boy who had a fight with his brother. They exploded at one another, and finally they stopped talking. At the end of the day, they still weren't speaking. Mom went to tuck one of the boys in bed, and she said, "Son, you've got to deal with this anger. You and your brother have to make up because the Bible says don't let the sun go down while you are still angry." To which the boy responded, "Mom, how am I going to keep the sun from going down?"[8]

Isn't that how many of us are? We want to hold on to our anger and never let go. But anger drives wedges between people that can destroy relationships. Tricia and I made a commitment early in our marriage that we would never go to bed angry. We have had some late nights along the way! It is important to deal with anger while it is still fresh and come to resolution before bitterness sets in.

How we talk to one another, how often we talk to one another, how we listen to one another, and how we respond to one another can either build a positive love connection or cause us to wake up one day and say I don't even feel like I know this person. We have to talk to one another. Communication is essential for an intimate love connection.

---

[8] Atchley, Making Room for Talk, audiotape

Touch

An intimate love connection will not take place without making deposits into your Love Bank of positive touches. I was watching a rerun episode of Everybody Loves Raymond recently, and Ray was being razzed by his brother that his marriage was not all it should be. Ray made a decision to try to work on his marriage by being more romantic. As Ray and his wife, Deborah, lay in bed together, he reached out and held her hand. Her response was to pull away and say not now Ray. He said, "What do you mean? I was just trying to hold your hand. I was trying to do something to help our marriage." She was moved and said, "Oh, you were trying to help our marriage? I thought you only wanted to have sex." Guys, our reputation precedes us. The way we are wired causes us to think of sex when we think of touch. And don't get me wrong, that is an important part! But there is so much more to it than simply sex. While most men think of intimacy as physical touch that leads to sexual union, women, on the other hand, tend to view physical intimacy as happening through simply holding one another, connecting with one another, and really looking into each other's eyes. I heard one woman define intimacy as into-me-see. Real intimacy happens through a real physical connection that includes more than sex. Guys, we need to be especially mindful of that because that doesn't come naturally for most of us.

Most of us tend to be about as sensitive to the importance of this as one guy I heard of who was concerned about how his wife had been acting recently, and so he took her to the doctor. The doctor gave the woman a complete physical. Afterwards he said to the man, "Your wife is completely fine." The man said, "Then why is she so listless? Why does she seem so depressed?" The doctor got up from behind his desk, walked around it, and gave the woman a huge hug and kissed her on the cheek. Immediately she brightened. The doctor looked at the husband and said, "She needs that three times a week!" To which the husband responded, "Well I could bring her in on Tuesdays and Thursdays, but Saturdays I play golf."

I really believe that a healthy marriage needs plenty of positive touch. In the same way that food provides nourishment for our physical health, so touch provides nourishment for our emotional and relational health. "Whatever there is of me resides in my body. To touch my body is to touch me. To withdraw from my body is to distance yourself from me emotionally."[9]

In talking to couples who have come to see me with marriage problems, I have found that this can be a huge issue. Many marriages are starving to death because of a lack of touch. When was the last time you simply sat and held your mate? When was the last time you walked holding hands? When was the last time you put your arms around each other and just sat close together and looked into each other's eyes? If we're going to make a lasting love connection, we've got to touch one another.

Transparency

One of the things I notice as I read the story of Adam and Eve is that when God first brought them together as husband and wife it was a transparent relationship. Genesis 2:25 says, "The man and his wife were both naked, and they felt no shame." Why was that? Adam and Eve had not yet sinned, and they didn't have to deal with any of the consequences of sin. There were no skeletons in their closet to hide from one another. There were no lies to be told to deceive one another. There were no inhibitions to keep them from fully relating to one another. There were also no jobs to overwork at, no friends to stay out late with, and no in-laws to deal with. It was a totally transparent relationship in every way.

---

[9] Gary Chapman, The Five Love Languages (Chicago: Northfield Publishing, 1992), 107.

Then Adam and Eve sinned. Eve listened to Satan, who was disguised as a serpent, and ate the fruit God had told them not to eat. She then convinced Adam to eat the fruit as well. And what was the result of their eating that fruit? "Then the eyes of both of them were opened, and they realized they were naked; so they sewed fig leaves together and made coverings for themselves," (Gen. 3:7). The result of sin was immediate inhibition in their dealings with one another. They were self-conscious. They covered themselves up. There was no longer the same transparency. And they hid from God. Sin had separated them from God and from one another.

Jesus came into this world to save us from the sin that alienates us from God and from one another so we can be transparent and experience intimacy. I really believe that when we surrender our lives to Jesus Christ and work to grow closer in our relationship with Him, that it will allow us to be more and more transparent with one another. The result will be that we will grow closer to one another. We will never be able to achieve the level of transparency that was present in the garden before Adam and Eve sinned, but the closer we get to God and the farther we get from sin, the more open, honest, uninhibited, and transparent we should become with one another. That is vital for a real love connection. You can't have real intimacy, real closeness with someone from whom you are hiding a bunch of secrets. God's intention has always been for a man and woman in a marriage relationship to be totally transparent with one another.

We are all looking for that lasting love connection. But it doesn't happen automatically. It takes huge investments of time. It takes communicating with one another by being quick to listen, slow to speak, and slow to become angry. It takes touching each other in positive ways that communicate important messages of how much you really love your mate. And it takes being totally transparent with each other, not hiding any secrets from your mate.

• •

Chapter 3

Charades

Understanding Your Role

I'm sure we've all played the ever-popular party game charades. In charades, you have to mimic different roles so the other people on your team can guess what you are trying to act out. In every marriage, God has given both husbands and wives unique roles to act out. When these roles are played properly, it will have a positive effect upon the marriage. When one or both spouses don't play the roles God intended them to play, or play the part their spouse is supposed to play, it can wreck havoc in a marriage relationship.

When God created man and woman and made them husband and wife, He created them uniquely—not only physically but in other ways as well. God told Adam when He made Eve, "I will make a helpmate who is suitable for you." She was to be a complement to him—not exactly like him but to help complete him. Please understand men and women are created equal by God. This does not mean, however, that their roles are to be the same.

I know what I'm about to say in this section is not a popular teaching today. I know this might be hard for some of you to read, but don't shoot the messenger! I have to share this with you for these reasons.

1. It's not my teaching. It's found in the Word of God.
2. It works. When a man and woman understand the unique roles
    that God has given them to fulfill in a marriage relationship
    and begin to live out those roles, it can have a huge, successful
    impact upon a marriage relationship.

The Husband's Role

While there are many responsibilities that a husband has to carry
out within a marriage, there are two primary roles that God has
designated for him to play within the marriage relationship.

Role No. 1: Leader

Perhaps you've heard the story of the guy who died and went
to heaven, and when he arrived outside the pearly gates, there were
two lines with signs above each one. The first sign read, "For men
who have been dominated by their wives all their lives." When the
guy looked at this line, he realized it stretched as far as he could see.
The second sign read, "For men who have never been dominated by
their wives during their lifetime." When he looked at this line, he
saw one solitary guy standing there. He decided to go talk to this guy
and said, "Let me shake your hand. You've never been dominated
by your wife in your life, how did you do it?" The guy said, "Look,
buddy, I don't even know why I'm in this line, but my wife told me
to stand here!"

We have all heard the jokes about the wife who wears the pants
in the family, but when you look at Scripture, it clearly indicates that
God has designated the husband to be the leader within the marriage
and family.

This is the role that most men seem to think of first when it
comes to marriage. We want our wives to know that God said, "We
are to be the leaders!" But, husbands, we need to understand that this
responsibility of leadership is a huge burden. And I did not say we

are called by God to be dictators, but rather leaders. As leaders, we have the responsibility, not to sit around and bark out orders, but to lead our wives, to set an example they'll want to follow, and motivate them to be the best they can be.

Again, I am well aware that this idea of the husband being the leader in the home is not a popular concept in today's society. But according to God's Word, that's the way it is supposed to be. "For the husband is the head of the wife as Christ is the head of the church, his body, of which he is the Savior," (Eph. 5:23). God knew for any organization to be successful, there had to be a designated leader. If there are two head coaches, team members don't know who to follow. If there are two CEOs of a corporation, employees wonder whose vision they are to respond to and implement for the company. In the home, there also needs to be a designated leader. God said it is to be the husband.

However, husbands, don't miss your model for leadership in the home. It's Jesus Christ. When you look at Jesus and His leadership of the church, it was not a dictatorship. It was servant leadership. He set an example for us. He didn't sit in heaven and bark out orders. He came to this earth, picked up a towel and basin, and served us. Over and over His leadership was marked by servanthood.

Servant leaders get involved. Servant leaders pick up the towel and basin and serve their families. Servant leaders lead on the front lines. They get down and dirty into the trenches of what needs to be done in their family. Husbands, we've got to be willing to do whatever it takes to serve our wives and children. If we sit around and bark out orders, we aren't going to be effective as leaders. If you choose to lead like that, you might get your wife and children to listen and obey, but in the process, you will crush their spirit and keep them from developing into all God intends for them to be. Again, men, understand that leadership is different than dictatorship. Leadership does not mean barking out orders. It means getting intimately involved in serving your wife and family. To put it another way, if you want the mantel of leadership, you've got to get into the trenches and lead by your example.

Many homes are disintegrating today for lack of a husband who wants to be leader. It is a real temptation for men to go to work and lead all day in the marketplace and come home at night and mentally check out. Everyday when I go to work, I have to be a leader of leaders within a fast-growing church. That's a lot of responsibility. And it's easy for me to come home at the end of the day, kick back in my La-Z-Boy, and be passive about what happens at home. I'm exhausted, and it's tempting to say to my wife, "You take care of leading the home. I've already got enough to do." Husbands, God has called us to lead. That means we have to be involved. We have to take initiative to help with the children, impart spiritual values to our families, deal with financial decisions, and set the tone for the direction of our family. God has given husbands that mantel of leadership, and it's a huge responsibility. There are many wives who would be willing to follow a husband who would get out there and lead, but I have found that many husbands instead of taking this God-given responsibility seriously want to check out and pass this mantel of leadership in the home off to their wife. That's not how God designed it to be.

Perhaps some men would say, "I've tried to lead but my wife won't allow me to lead." I'm confident, men, if our leadership is marked by servanthood, our wives would be willing to follow. That's what God calls us to do within our marriages. We must, first of all, lead our wives.

Role No. 2: Lover

"Husbands, love your wives, just as Christ loved the church and gave himself up for her," (Eph. 5:25). Husbands, this is not a suggestion. This is not a recommendation. This is a command. You are to love your wife. Notice how you are to love your wife—"as Christ loved the church." How did Christ love the church? By giving Himself up for her. His love was demonstrated by self-sacrifice. He set aside His own rights for us. He sacrificed the glory of heaven to come to earth for us. He gave up His life on a cross for us. He didn't demand His own way but rather set aside Himself to do what was best for us. Men, that should be the way we love our wives as well. If we want to love our wives the way Jesus loved the church, we have to be willing to sacrifice ourselves for her.

If that means giving up something we really want to do for something she really wants to do, we should be willing to do it. If that means turning off the television so we can have some time for conversation, we should be willing to do it. It's a sacrificial love.

Guys, I have to be honest. I still struggle with this. It is so easy for me to simply focus on what I want to do and not on the needs of my wife. I love to play golf and one of the hot button issues for us over the years has been how much time it takes to play a round of golf. For me, I look at golf and say, "I need that! It's relaxing for me." Tricia looks at golf and says, "What a waste of time! Why wouldn't you rather be home with me?" What I have had to do is to learn to be sensitive. When I play golf, I will often play early in the morning so I can be home with her the rest of the day. Or, if it has been especially busy and I know I haven't been home much, I have learned that's probably a good time for me to put the needs of my wife before my own desire to play golf. For me that's sacrificial love!

The way Christ loved the church was not only a sacrificial love but an unconditional love. Jesus doesn't say I love you if . . . , or I love you when . . . , He simply says I love you, period. It's an unconditional love. Husbands are called to love their wives unconditionally as well. In your marriage vows you said, "I take you." Notice there were no conditions given with that vow. It was not, "I take you if" or "I will take you when." No you simply said, "I take you." And by that you were saying, "I take you the way you are." When you agreed to take her as your wife, you agreed to take her as she was. There are going to be positive things about her that will bless your life, and there will be some things you will probably struggle with. But you choose to love her in spite of those things. You love her unconditionally, without comparing, without complaining, without criticizing, and without abuse.

This love really ought to be evident in the way you treat your wife. First Peter 3:7 says, "Husbands, in the same way be considerate as you live with your wives, and treat them with respect as the weaker partner and as heirs with you of the gracious gift of life, so that nothing will hinder your prayers." Today many would say it's sexist to say the wife is the weaker vessel, but I don't believe it is at all. Let me give you an example. For every-day dinner, most of us don't use our best china, do we? We use cheaper dinnerware. And if we have young children, we probably give them plates that are plastic, sturdy, and unbreakable. Who cares if they get marked up, beat up, or even if they get broken? They can easily be replaced. But china that is delicate and precious, we save for special occasions. When we use it, we know it's valuable, so we treat it with special care.

I think that's what Peter is saying. "Husbands, demonstrate your love to your wife in the way you treat her, because she is a most valuable treasure." She is that delicate china. I heard Zig Ziglar say one time, "If you treat your wife like a thoroughbred, she will seldom act like a nag." Treat your wife with respect, treat her like a thoroughbred. Communicate your love by holding the door open for her, not slamming it in her face. Pay attention when she is talking to you; don't stare off into space unresponsively. Tell your wife you love her; don't assume she already knows. Put your arm around her or hold her hand; don't be shy about displaying your love for her publicly. Do what it takes to communicate how valuable she is to you.

Those are the two primary roles I see for the husband in the Bible. Men, we are called to be leaders and lovers. And if you fulfill your role by leading and loving as Jesus led and loved, I think you will be amazed at how responsive your wife will be.

The Wife's Role

God has blessed me with a wonderful wife who understands and lives out her God-given role. So I have asked my wife, Tricia, to write this section on the role of the wife.

I have been married for over fifteen years and am continually learning and growing as a wife. I don't think we ever reach a point where we finally have it all figured out. What I do know is that God is the author of creativity and He has a sense of humor! He has created all of us uniquely, and it seems that he places two completely opposite personalities together in a marriage. Todd and I attended a marriage conference early in our marriage where we took a personality assessment. We found that our personalities are totally and completely opposite—on the far ends of the spectrum. We can't be any more different! The funny thing is all but one couple at the conference found out the same thing. Because most of us are so opposite from our spouses, sometimes we don't understand each other and conflicts can arise. We need to discover and appreciate our husband's unique, God-given personality and understand our own unique role in order to become a Godly wife.

I wholeheartedly believe being a good wife starts with your own relationship with God. Elizabeth George, in A Wife after God's Own Heart, says, "The most important thing you must decide to do each and every day as a wife is to put the Lord first."[1] God knows us intimately, and it is only by staying in constant communication with Him that we can have a wonderful and fulfilling marriage. Studying God's Word daily, obeying what it says, and turning everything over to God in prayer is essential to maintaining a close relationship with our Lord. I encourage you to find a study which appeals to you where you are and dive into God's Word.

[1] Elizabeth George, A Wife after God's Own Heart (Eugene, OR: Harvest House Publishers, 2004), 18.

I have heard many women say they don't have time. I know; I am the queen of excuses. I was challenged in a woman's Bible study years ago to get up early in the morning before the kids and spend time studying and praying. I did it, and it literally changed my life. I now look forward to that time in the morning with my Bible, my God, and my coffee! Now, don't get me wrong, there are times when I'm lazy and don't get up. Those are usually the days where everything goes wrong and I feel completely frazzled. I believe if we strive toward spiritual growth in our own lives, we will reap God's blessings in our marriage. How? Your behavior will change as you become more Christ-like and your relationship with your husband will change as a result.

It is also important to embrace our uniqueness as a woman and as a wife. Genesis 2:18 says, "The Lord God said, 'It is not good for the man to be alone. I will make a helper suitable for him'." We see in this verse that God thought man needed a partner, so He created someone perfectly suited to meet that need. Then in Genesis 1:27, the Bible says, "So God created man in his own image, in the image of God he created him; male and female he created them." We are unique creations of God, totally different from men but also made in God's image. This thought alone should make us feel like a princess. We need to be careful about our self-worth coming from things or people. When we focus on our relationship with our King and how special we are to Him, we can feel like a princess no matter what the world says. Proverbs 18:22 says, "He who finds a wife finds what is good and receives favor from the Lord."

We also need to be aware of what the Bible says about our responsibilities in the marriage relationship and commit to obeying God's commands whether or not our husband is obedient in his responsibilities as the husband. We are only answerable to God for our own actions, not the actions of our husband. Only he is answerable for his actions. This means that we cannot rely on the excuse that we would be a better wife if only our husband would step up to the plate. I want to encourage you, even if your husband is not fulfilling his God-given role, to be obedient to what God has revealed to you. You never know how your obedience might affect your husband. So what exactly does the Bible say about the wife's responsibilities in a marriage?

The most talked about and least popular role that God calls for a wife to fulfill is submission. This is a role of the wife that God unquestionably has laid out in his Word. Colossians 3:18 says, "Wives, submit to your husbands, as is fitting in the Lord." How many of you cringe when you read this? This verse has caused much controversy in this age of women's lib. Frankly, I think it's because of the way it has been interpreted. We get a picture in our mind of a quiet, meek, passive, dull, and boring existence with a husband whose main job is to keep us under his thumb. That is not at all what God has called us to be as a wife. I cannot believe that God created women with incredible talents, gifts, and passionate personalities and then expects us to live lives completely squelched by our husbands. Instead, I believe that God placed us in a partnership with our husbands to be his helper. As one person has so perfectly stated, submission is to be "under our husband's mission." I think that a wife can do whatever she desires as long as it falls within her husband's mission for their family and she has his blessing. A practical way we can show submission to our husband can be to let our husband make a final decision on an issue—even when we think he is wrong. You should not be afraid of the word "submit." If we are obedient in this area, God will bless our marriage.

Now let me make something clear. There are occasionally times when a husband may ask a wife to do something that is contrary to God's moral standards. In these situations, your primary obedience needs to be to the Lord. But in the vast majority of circumstances that is not the case and we need to be willing to allow him to be the leader God designed him to be.

Helping is another role of the wife that God has commanded. In Genesis 2:18 the Bible says, "The Lord God said, 'It is not good for the man to be alone. I will make a helper suitable for him'." God created us to be a helper for our husband. We tend to think of this role as second best, but the roles of helping and leading are equally valued in Scripture. One is not more important than the other. A helper requires that a leader be present, and a leader requires that a helper be present. I have heard it said many times that behind every good man there is a good woman. We all want our husbands to be successful and confident, and by being a good helper to our husbands, we can help them be just that. We can free our husband to be the leader he is called to be by being the helper we are called to be. We also help our husbands with a positive, willing attitude. If we help him grudgingly, it will create resentment in us toward our spouse. Some practical ways to help our husband are to create a warm and loving home environment, to be a good home manager, and to pray for our husband and to let him know that we are praying for him.

We are also called to respect our husbands. The Amplified Bible says in Ephesians 5:33, "And let the wife see that she respects and reverences her husband—that she notices him, regards him, honors him, prefers him, venerates and esteems him exceedingly." Respecting your husband involves understanding and appreciating the weight of his responsibilities and pressures and his unique needs as a man. Encouragement and admiration both demonstrate respect to your husband. If you respect your husband, it will give him confidence, and it will energize and motivate him. Even if your husband is not being "respectable," you can respect his God-given position in your marriage.

The last role of the wife that I see from Scripture is to love our husbands. Titus 2:4 says, "Encourage the young women to love their husbands," (NASB). Making love is more than sex. Love is an attitude of unconditional acceptance. Part of loving our husbands is being aware of what his needs are and determining how to meet those needs effectively. In Willard Harley's book His Needs, Her Needs, he lists the five top needs of most men—sexual fulfillment, recreational companionship, an attractive spouse, domestic support, and admiration.[2] Not all men have these same needs. Remember that God has created every individual uniquely. The best way to find out what your husband's unique needs as a man are is to ask him! Don't try to analyze him and figure it out yourself. It is common for us to think that our needs are the same as our husbands, but in most cases our husband's needs are totally different from ours. It is our responsibility as a wife to find out what our husband's needs are and to try to meet those needs to the best of our ability.

I've heard many women say, "Well, if he would start meeting my needs, it would be a lot easier to want to meet his needs." While that may be true, we cannot wait for our husband to meet our needs before we meet his. That approach ends in isolation and resentment. If he is not meeting our needs, we need to start meeting his needs anyway. It is amazing to watch how a person thrives when his or her needs are being met in the marriage relationship. Once that happens, the person will usually begin to desire to meet their spouse's needs.

The best definition of what true love is can be found in 1 Corinthians 13:4–8, "Love is patient, love is kind. It does not envy, it does not boast, it is not proud. It is not rude, it is not self-seeking, it is not easily angered, it keeps no record of wrongs. Love does not delight in evil but rejoices with the truth. It always protects, always trusts, always hopes, always perseveres. Love never fails." If we keep in mind what true love really is, it will help us in our role as a wife. If we love our husbands, it will be easier for us to submit to, help, and respect our husbands.

---

[2] Harley, His Needs, Her Needs, 12.

· ·

Chapter 4

Family Feud
Dealing with Conflict

W hen I was a kid, I remember watching reruns of *Father Knows Best*. That show depicted a perfect family. It starred actor Robert Young, who played John Anderson, the tender husband and father of three. Each week, he would guide his family with wit, wisdom, and patience through some type of problem that could be easily solved in the course of thirty minutes. Robert Young, it seemed could handle anything. In the comfort of our living rooms, we watched as he held his family together while avoiding the pain of conflict.

But that was television. Off the set, I understand that Robert Young was leading a troubled life. He was an alcoholic, prone to violence and depression. While the character on the screen, John Anderson, was happy and functional, the actor, Robert Young, was sad and dysfunctional. He hurt others and himself deeply.[1]

There are too many homes that mirror this sad story. There are too many families who display themselves to the world as peaceful

---

[1] www.cnn.com/showbiz/TV/9807/22/obit.young

and functional, but behind closed doors, there is painful conflict. The truth is every family has conflict to a certain extent. No family is perfect because every family is comprised of mere mortals—imperfect people. Every family feuds and needs to deal with conflict at some time and at some level. Feuds will happen in every marriage. Feuds will happen in every family. It's how we handle these battles that determines whether we can live together in peace and harmony or whether the battle becomes an all out war filled with bloodshed that leaves family members suffering in its wake.

Let's begin with the basic premise that all families feud. There are no perfect marriages or perfect families. Therefore, every family needs to be equipped for conflict resolution. The Bible reminds us how important this is, "A home filled divided against itself is doomed," (Mark 3:25 NLT).

Why do we have conflict? The Bible is very blunt about this. There is only one reason for conflict in relationships, whether within marriage, the family or any other area of our lives. "What causes fights and quarrels among you? Don't they come from your desires that battle within you?" (James 4:1). The real reason we experience conflict is because we have competing desires. I want what I want, and you want what you want, and we can't both have it our way, and so there is conflict. I have found that by nature I'm a self-centered person. I have desires within, things that I want to happen the way I want them to happen, and when someone interferes with my desires, I can get a little edgy. And you know what? So can you! That's where the vast majority of our conflicts come from.

It's how we respond when these conflicts come that can cause our relationships to be built up or torn down. Here are some common responses to conflict that I have observed.

Response No. 1: "I will win." For some people, every fight becomes a contest they must win. They are competitive. They think, I will assert my will until you give in to my demands.

I'm totally right. You're totally wrong. And I will prove it to you by winning this fight. Some of you reading this probably recognize yourselves. You fight in this same way. You are stubborn, bullheaded, and will keep going until you wear the other person down and win the fight.

Response No. 2: "I will run." Some people say, "I hate conflict. I don't want to deal with it. I will avoid conflict at all costs." They run away. Here's the problem. While this person may be peaceful to live with, this can create deeper problems because they suppress their feelings. They never really deal with the issues behind the problems, and so nothing gets resolved.

Response No. 3: "I will give in." Some people give in to every battle. They don't run from the conflict, but they're the golden retriever who can't stand that the other person may be upset with them, and so they roll over and play dead. The thinking here is, I want your approval. I want to make you happy, so I'll pretend I'm a doormat. I'll always give in to your wishes." Again this person may be peaceful to live with, but they're probably not very happy because they always give in and never express their own thoughts and feelings.

Response No. 4: "I will compromise." These people like to find the middle ground in every battle. They say, "I'll meet you half way. I'll give a little; you give a little. I'll win some; you win some. Let's come up with a compromise we both can live with." This is better than the first three ways of dealing with conflict, but it is still not the best way.

Response No. 5: "I will reconcile." This is someone who says, "I'm not only interested in solving this problem, but in strengthening our relationship as well." That's the best way to deal with conflict. Not to simply compromise, but to put the relationship first and do everything we can to strengthen it. I have found that this is not only the best way to deal with conflict but the hardest way as well. I am by nature a competitive person, so when Tricia and I have conflict, I find myself wanting to win. But I've had to learn over the years, that I love Tricia more than I love winning, and so I need to be willing to do what it takes to reconcile and prioritize the relationship over the satisfaction of personal victory. How does this happen?

How can we deal with conflicts in a way that honors God, brings resolution to the problem, and reconciles the relationship as well?

Put God First

I am talking about a Christian marriage here. If you have not yet committed your life to Christ and made Him not only the Lord of your life but Lord of your marriage as well, you need to start there. I know that sounds like a Sunday school answer, but before you tune me out, read carefully. Before you can deal effectively with any other conflict in your life, whether it is conflict with your spouse, your kids, or anyone else, you have to first resolve the conflict that exists between yourself and God. You might wonder what this has to do with resolving feuds in your marriage or family. It has everything to do with it! The Bible tells us that every single person is made in God's image. And the purpose of God making us and placing us on this earth is so that we can experience an intimate love relationship with Him that is real and personal. But here's the problem. We have all sinned against God. When we chose to sin, it drove a wedge in our relationship with God and put us as an enemy of God. The Bible says because of this sin, we are at war with God. You may or may not feel it, but it's the absolute truth. Our sin has separated us from God, and we are in conflict with Him. Jesus put it this way, "He who is not for me is against me." There is no middle ground. You can't say, "God, you stay on your side of the fence, and I'll stay on my side, and we'll have truce with each other." It doesn't work that way. Jesus says if you are not for Me, you are against Me. So until we settle that conflict with God, it's going to spill out into conflict with others.

How do we settle this conflict with God? We confess our sin and receive Jesus Christ as our Savior. When that happens, we are reconciled to God. We are no longer at war with Him. Until this happens in your life, you will always find yourself with unresolved conflict. The starting point in resolving conflict with anyone else is to first come to the cross and reconcile your relationship with God through committing to Jesus Christ. I am 100 percent convinced that most marriage conflicts could be solved overnight if both the husband and wife would get down on their knees and say, "Yes, God. I surrender my life to You. I want to put you first in this relationship. Teach us how to reconcile these conflicts."

Why would that make a difference? Because if Jesus is in you and Jesus is in me, He will not fight with Himself, will He? Additionally, when we surrender our lives to Jesus Christ, we receive the gift of the Holy Spirit. God comes to take up residency within us. And the Bible says the fruit of the Spirit is love, joy, peace, patience, kindness, goodness, faithfulness, gentleness, and self-control. If both husband and wife have surrendered to Jesus Christ as Savior and have been filled with the Holy Spirit, then they should be helped to reconcile by the character traits the Spirit has developed within them. If my life is producing fruit as a byproduct of having the Holy Spirit in me and my wife is also producing the same fruit because the Spirit is in her, this will have a huge impact upon resolving conflict in relationships.

So, first of all, resolve this conflict with God and recognize your primary purpose on this earth is to relate to Him. You will never adequately be able to deal with your conflicts with others until you first of all get this conflict with God cleared up.

Pray About It

Once you have committed your life to Christ, you no longer have to deal with conflict by your own power. You have an open line of communication with God where you can take your issues and problems to Him. Yet I have found that many times even believers will still try to deal with their problems on their own. If you are still trying to handle things yourself until it gets really bad and you have to turn to God, I want to encourage you to stop doing that. Prayer is one of the greatest untapped resources we have for resolving conflicts. Take the issue to God. Pray about it. In fact, when you face conflict, learn to make this your first response. Before you even talk to your mate, or whoever else you might be in conflict with, talk to God. You know what I have found to be true? When I talk to God about why I'm upset or angry, that often settles the issue right there. I sometimes hear the Holy Spirit clearly reveal to me that it's mostly my problem anyway and I'm the one who needs to change. "You quarrel and fight. You do not have, because you do not ask God," (James 4:2). Notice James says, "Ask God." We all need to learn to take our anger and frustration to God first. We're really good at sharing our anger and frustration with the people around us, but often we fail to take it to God and talk with him about it. So when you face conflict, make prayer your first step in dealing with the issue.

Practice Meeting the Needs of Your Mate

Once you have prayed about the situation, I encourage you to ask yourself, what does my mate need from me right now? Here's why. We often create the conflict we face because our entire focus is on the unholy trinity of me, myself, and I. Ask yourself, "Why am I really upset? Is it because I am focusing first on my own needs, my own hurts, my own desires? Do I need to shift my focus to meet the needs of my spouse?" If you find you are focusing primarily on yourself, try shifting your focus. Put yourself in the other person's position, and ask yourself what you can do to meet their needs, their hurts, and their desires.

The Bible says in Philippians 2:3, "Regard one another as more important than yourselves," (NASB). Here's the problem with that verse for me. It's the phrase one another. Most of us think of ourselves as being the most important person in our lives. What happens when we don't get what we want? We get angry, and we find ourselves in the middle of a conflict, and it's because we are preoccupied with ourselves. All we can see is our own hurts, wants, and desires. Anger is self-centered most of the time. But if we learn to switch that focus and ask ourselves, "What are my mate's needs? What can I do for him/her right now?" it would change the whole complexion of the argument.

Here are three little phrases that I would highly recommend you use to reduce the level of tension in any conflict. "I am sorry." "I was only thinking of myself." "Will you forgive me?" After you pick your spouse up off the floor from fainting, you can work at resolving the real issues!

Pursue Reconciliation Not Necessarily Resolution

Once you've settled your conflict with God, prayed about the issue, and removed the focus from yourself and paid attention to the needs of your spouse, then and only then are you ready to sit down and talk about the situation. Now here's the kicker. There are times you will not resolve the situation. Resolution means settling every issue. That's not always possible or realistic. You and your mate come from different backgrounds. You have different perspectives. There are going to be times when you will have legitimate differences in how you see things. That's okay. That does not mean the relationship is doomed! The reason? You can have reconciliation without having resolution. You can reconcile the relationship without resolving every issue. Reconciliation means that even though you don't settle every issue, you are going to prioritize the relationship over the issue. Reconciliation means you bury the hatchet, not the issue. You can keep talking about it, but you do it in a spirit of love and harmony. It really is possible to walk arm in arm without seeing eye to eye.

There's a great verse in the Bible to remember when you are pursuing reconciliation. Ephesians 4:29 says, "Do not use harmful words, but only helpful words, the kind that build up and provide what is needed, so that what you say will do good to those who hear you," (TEV). In other words, think before you speak and make sure your words are not going to throw gasoline on the fire instead of water. I often get into trouble when I do this. When I respond in anger, I hurt, not help, the situation. Make sure your words are helpful and not harmful. You can have reconciliation without having resolution of every problem.

Let me mention that there are times when conflicts have gone on so long and the wounds are so deep that you may need help in bringing reconciliation. When you are stuck in conflict and you can't seem to get anywhere, I want to encourage you to set your pride aside and go seek godly counsel. In every other area of life when we face big problems, we're not afraid to seek professional help, are we? If we are sick physically, we go to the doctor. If we have tax issues, we call a CPA. If we have a legal problem, we call an attorney. But when we get stuck in relational problems in our marriages, our pride keeps us from seeking help. I want to challenge you, when it gets to this point, set aside your pride and seek help. Find a Christian mentor couple who has been through this situation before who can help walk you through it. Go to a Christian counselor who can give you godly advice for conflict resolution. And do it immediately! Don't put it off. Don't keep wearing the mask publicly and pretending everything is okay while privately your marriage is crumbling apart. The bottom line is, do you want to really have a satisfying marriage or do you want to only pretend that you have one? If you really want to have a satisfying marriage, there are times you have to swallow your pride and seek outside help. That can be difficult. Swallowing our pride always is. It may mean walking through some tough issues you'd rather ignore. But it's always more rewarding to resolve a conflict than to dissolve a relationship.[2]

---

[2] Adapted from Tom Holladay, How to Resolve Conflict, audiotape (Lake Forest, CA: The Encouraging Word Tape Ministry).

Chapter 5

Monopoly

For Love or Money

I enjoy playing Monopoly. It has been a standing tradition that when my family gets together, we have a big Monopoly game. My boys love it, but my wife hates it. She won't play with us because we turn into exceptionally competitive people, trying to invest our money and win. We can sometimes be obnoxious. While Monopoly is simply a financial game that some of us enjoy playing, I know many adults who play with their finances as though they were playing with Monopoly money.

Many people simply spend money with no plan. They carry cash in their wallet and spend it without knowing where it went, and then when the wallet runs dry, they turn to the ATM machine for more cash or start charging purchases on a credit card. Many people charge vacations, Christmas presents, furniture, and all sorts of miscellaneous expenditures. They continue to do it, even when they know there is no money there to cover the purchases, thus running up an alarming amount of debt. At some point, however, the bills come due. A medical emergency or a car accident occurs, and they are pushed to the financial brink, causing even more marital problems.

Nothing causes more disharmony in a marriage than how finances are used or abused. When you read the marriage manuals and divorce statistics, financial problems top the list of reasons why couples fight or why marriages come to an end. This is a real problem. It becomes a power struggle in some families.

One of the key reasons that many of us get into this kind of financial mess is that we have bought into the thinking that permeates our American mindset today—if you have more things, you will be more satisfied. Solomon clearly refutes this as a myth. "Whoever loves money never has money enough; whoever loves wealth is never satisfied with his income. This too is meaningless," (Eccles. 5:10). What's Solomon saying? You can't buy satisfaction. Your yearning power will always exceed your earning power. If you want to know if you've ever bought into this myth, ask yourself this question. Have you ever thought or said, "I don't want to be rich, I only want enough to _____ (you fill in the blank)." What are you saying? If I had a little more, I could be a little more satisfied. But it's a myth. Solomon says you will never be satisfied, even if you have a little bit more.

What's the solution? It's to learn to handle finances according to God's plan. If we want to win in this game, we can't treat finances like Monopoly money. We need to learn to follow God's principles for financial management.

God's Principles for Financial Management

Principle # 1 God Owns It All

The first thing that we have to get straight if we are going to handle finances according to God's wisdom is the principle of ownership. Whose money do we have in our pockets? Who does it belong to? It belongs to God. Ownership starts with God and not you. God is the owner of all things. We are simply the stewards, or managers, of His things. Anything you say that you own, you don't really own, you simply manage. It is the property of another. It is the property of God. There is probably no doctrine in the Bible more clearly taught than this one. It's the very first doctrine of the Bible, "In the beginning God created the heavens and the earth," (Gen. 1:1). Let me paraphrase it for you; God made it all, so it ain't yours, it's His. If you are still struggling with understanding this, let me share a few more verses: Exodus 19:5, God says, "The whole earth is mine;" Psalm 89:11, "The heavens are yours, and yours also the earth; you founded the world and all that is in it;" Psalm 50:11, "I know every bird in the mountains, and the creatures of the field are mine;" 1 Corinthians 10:26, "The earth is the Lord's, and everything in it;" 1 Corinthians 6:19, "Do you not know that your body is a temple of the Holy Spirit, who is in you, whom you have received from God? You are not your own." In other words, even your body doesn't belong to you but to God. The Bible makes no apologies in reminding us time and again who we work for. The Bible doesn't hesitate for one single minute to remind you that everything you touch in life doesn't belong to you. It is owned by someone else. It is owned by God. Nothing you touch belongs to you. You want the ultimate proof of that? Everything you touch in life will one day do one of two things:

- It will leave you. If will rust, wear out, be stolen, or sold to someone else.
- Or you will leave it. You will die.

Those are the only two options. Now I understand we use that term "my" when talking about the possessions we manage. I say "my house," but in reality it is not my house. Someday it will leave my possession or I will leave it by leaving this earth. I say "my car," but it's not really my car. Someday it will wear out or I will get tired of it and sell it to another's possession or I will die and leave it for someone else to drive. We own nothing in the absolute sense. And before we can be good family financial managers, we have to understand our role, we are simply managers. We have a trust and a responsibility to manage the things God blesses us with in a responsible way.

Principle # 2 Put God First

One of the ways you acknowledge God's ownership is to give Him back the tithe, the first 10 percent, trusting God to meet all the rest of your needs. "The purpose of tithing is to teach you always to put God first in your lives," (Deut. 14:23 TLB). God is saying, "I want you to put me first in your life and acknowledge that I am the owner of all things, and here's how you do it, you give me the tithe."

I learned this lesson the hard way. Shortly after I got out of college, I went to work for an evangelist organization where our salary came from the support that we were able to raise. It was a tough way to make a living, especially for young guy right out of college. But I asked for support from all my relatives, friends, people I had gone to church with and raised what I could. However, the amount that I was able to raise was far short of what I needed to pay my bills. So I made a decision to stop tithing. I justified it because I was doing God's work. Surely He would understand. This was the first time in my life that I had not tithed. My parents had taught me to tithe from my very first allowance. But now I thought I couldn't afford it. I went through a year of absolute financial misery. I was short of being able to pay my bills. I had to juggle what ones I was going to pay and not pay. I went further in debt to be able to survive. And I started to get angry with God, too. I wondered, "God how could You let me be in such bad shape financially? After all, I'm serving You!" While it was not an audible voice, I very clearly heard God respond to me, "Todd, you're not putting Me first." I made a commitment from that day forward to begin to tithe. What I began to witness God do was absolutely amazing. While on paper, I still did not have enough money committed to cover my bills, I saw month after month for the next three years, God provide for me clearly. There were times when extra money would come in that was not committed. I had someone donate a car to my ministry so that I no longer had a car payment. I moved into a new place to live where my payment was about 1/3 of what it had been before. God proved His faithfulness to me. When I put Him first, He took care of all of my needs.

Now you couldn't stop me from tithing. Today, every time I get paid, I sit down and write a check to give that first 10 percent back to God. When I do that, it is an acknowledgment that everything I have comes from Him, and I want Him to have first place in every area of my life, including the finances He has entrusted to my care. The Bible is clear, when you put God first in the tithe, He promises to bless you and meet all of your needs. "'Bring the whole tithe into the storehouse, that there may be food in my house. Test me in this,' says the Lord Almighty, 'and see if I will not throw open the floodgates of heaven and pour out so much blessing that you will never have enough room for it,'" (Mal. 3:10). God says, "I dare you! Test Me by bringing Me the tithe! Trust Me and allow Me to meet your needs."

Some of you may be thinking, Our finances are tight already. There is no way we can afford to give God the first 10 percent. Every time I hear that thinking, my response is that you can't afford not to. Do you want to live under an open heaven or a closed heaven? Do you want to live under the blessing of God on the finances He entrusts to your care, or do you want to try to struggle by on your own? I am absolutely amazed how many people say they trust God with their salvation but then can't trust God with the tithe. How can you trust God with your eternal future if you can't trust Him to provide for your needs in your immediate future? Put God first and He will take care of you.

In fact, there's a life principle that I would mention here that you need to understand. Whatever you want God to bless, put Him first in it. Do you want God to bless your marriage? Put Him first in it. Do you want God to bless your business? Put Him first in it. Do you want God to bless your friendships? Put Him first in them. Do you want God to bless your finances? Put Him first in them. This is absolutely foundational to successful financial management.

Principle # 3 Budget Your Income

I know budget is a bad word for many people, but if you ignore this principle you will always have financial problems. I am most grateful that when I was in college, in our Practical Ministries class, a gentleman came in one day to teach us how to put together a budget. He taught us what he called the shoe box method. He told us to take an old shoe box and put an envelope in it for every bill we needed to pay and then every time we got paid to put enough money in each envelope so that when the bill came due we would have the money there to pay it. I used this "shoebox method" for several years. It was so simple and yet it worked so well. It was such a relief to know that every time a bill came due, I had the money for it because I hadn't spent the money on something else.

Today, I have replaced the shoe box with a computer, and I use a spreadsheet to do the very same thing. I still put into each budget category what amount needs to go there every time I get paid. This is something the Bible tells us we ought to do. "Plan carefully and you will have plenty; if you act too quickly, you will never have enough," (Prov. 21:5 TEV). God says make sure you plan your spending.

What is planned spending? It's a budget. You ought to know what you take in and where it goes. I am absolutely amazed how many people don't do this. They get paid, deposit the check, and spend it wherever they want. When the bills come due, they wonder where it all went. I heard someone say once, "My money used to talk; now it just flies away." If your money just flies away and you don't know where it goes, you will find yourself under constant financial pressure.

Some of you say, it's too restricting to do a budget or you don't have time to track all your spending. But the truth is if you would spend as much time doing your budget as you do worrying about it, then you would have a whole lot less to worry about and your stress levels would drop immensely. Not only are we talking about your personal stress levels, we are talking about the stress in your marriage. If marriages are ending because of financial stress, then you need to do what you can to reduce that stress, and budgeting will help immensely.

When you budget, it will also help you fight the urge to impulse buy. Impulse buying drives our economy. Have you ever bought anything on impulse? It's Friday night and you're bored. You go to the mall, and the next thing you know you've dropped $150 or $200 on miscellaneous items you didn't really need. When the bill comes, you don't have the money to pay it because it wasn't in your budget. It's okay to budget miscellaneous money for impulse times, but when the money is not there, you've got to learn to say no and not touch money that has been designated for other things.

Principle # 4 Borrow Money Cautiously

Living on borrowed money is so common in our society that most of us don't think much about it. I heard someone say the average person in America drives on a bond-financed highway, in a bank-financed car, fueled by credit-card-charged gasoline, going to purchase furniture on the installment plan, to decorate his mortgaged home! While we smile at that, the reality is it's a true description of where most of us find ourselves. We live in a society that promotes instant gratification. You can have it all, and you can have it all now! Charge it today, take it home, and after seventy-two easy payments, it will be yours. The reality is there is no such thing as easy payments. They are all hard. While it may be fun and satisfying to have it all instantly for awhile, pretty soon that newness wears off and the satisfaction diminishes, yet the difficult payments are still there. That new car is wonderful for awhile, but three years later, when it's only half paid for and repairs need to be done and you're ready for something different, it's not quite so exciting. Charging Christmas presents makes for a wonderful day of fun and joy for the kids, but December's excesses lead to January's payments, and it's not so fun anymore. "The rich rule over the poor, and the borrower is servant to the lender," (Prov. 22:7). The Bible strongly discourages debt because every time you go into it, you make yourself a servant to the lender.

I'll let you in on a little secret. Credit card companies aren't in business to lose money. They want you to buy now and pay slowly. I have watched many couples put things on credit cards that they really don't need right now but can't wait for, and soon they have a mountain of debt to deal with. Then it becomes a situation where both husband and wife have to work to pay the bills, and the stress becomes unbearable. It easily could break up a marriage. "It is for freedom that Christ has set us free," (Gal. 5:1). This verse is written in the context of legalism and not being a slave to the law, but it reminds us of a principle that appears throughout the Bible. God wants his people to be free. He doesn't want us to be a slave to anger. He doesn't want us to be a slave to immorality. He doesn't want us to be a slave to sin. And he doesn't want us to be a slave to debt. He wants us to be free from the constant anxiety of whether or not we can pay our debtors. He wants us to be free from the constant tension that exists in many marriages and homes.

Principle # 5 Save for the Future

"Take a lesson from the ants, you lazybones. Learn from their ways and be wise! Even though they have no prince, governor, or ruler to make them work, they labor hard all summer, gathering food for the winter," (Prov, 6:6–8 NLT). When we don't follow a budget and we fall prey to easy credit, we overextend ourselves to the point where everything that comes in must go out, and there is no saving for the future. But God's Word says we should take a lesson from the ant. They store up in the summer for the winter. In other words, don't spend it all now. There will come cold months in your financial future where things aren't as lucrative as they are today. If you haven't planned ahead and saved for those times, you will easily get into trouble. Now some people might say, "I don't feel I need to save. I should just trust God to take care of the future." It's true that as Christian people we ought to walk by faith and trust God for the future, but don't confuse trusting God to take care of your future with presumption upon God. You can't live carelessly and disregard God's principles for money management, which clearly include saving for the future, and then expect God to bail you out. That's not living by faith. That's living by disobedience and asking God to bless your disobedience. Proverbs 21:20 sums it up, "The wise man saves for the future, but the foolish man spends whatever he gets," (TLB).

Let me wrap up this section with an amazing story about how following God's financial principles can lead to a blessed life. It's from financial counselor Ron Blue's book Mastering Your Money. He tells about meeting a retired pastor who never earned more than $8,000 in one year. He met this humble man because he wanted to talk to him about whether or not he had enough financial resources to live out the rest of his life. At the time of his question, he was eighty years old; he had been retired for twenty years; and his wife and recently been put in a full-time nursing facility. Ron began the conversation by asking, "Do you have any debt?" The man's response was, "No. I never borrowed money because I knew I would have to pay it back someday, and I knew I couldn't afford to pay off debt, feed my family, and tithe." Ron then asked a second question. "What resources do you presently have?" The man told him that in his wife's name, they had a CD that was worth about $250,000, and in his name, they had a CD worth about $350,000. Ron was impressed. Over $600,000 accumulated by a couple who never made more than $8,000 in one year! The man went on to reveal that when he retired, he invested $10,000 in stock for a new company as well. And the present market

value was $1,063,000![1] How was this guy so successful? He followed
God's principles. He lived within his means, stayed out of debt, tithed
off every bit of his income, and saved for the future.

God's principles work! Remember, you do play the game of
Monopoly, but it's not just a game. The money you are using is not
play money, it's for real. And the way you use what God has entrusted
to your care can often make or break your marriage relationship.

---

[1] Ron Blue, Mastering Your Money (Nashville: Thomas Nelson Publishers,
1986), 13-14

Chapter 6

Sorry

Learning to Seek and Offer Forgiveness

N o matter how hard we try to work at keeping conflicts to a minimum and resolving them as quickly as possible, there are going to be times when the hurt has been great and forgiveness is necessary. Learning to seek and offer forgiveness are absolutely critical elements in any successful marriage. Why? Because no relationship will survive without forgiveness. Forgiveness sustains relationships. I guarantee you can not live up close and personal with someone day in and day out, year after year, and not experience hurt. At some point your spouse, or family member, will offend you, fail you, or become angry with you.

Lewis Smedes, in his book Forgive and Forget, tells of a woman named Jane and her husband, Ralph, who had finally gotten their children through the crazy maze of adolescence. When the kids were graduated and gone, Jane was relieved. She would finally have a life of her own and make something of herself. But family tragedy interrupted her plans. Ralph's younger brother and his wife were killed in a car crash. They left behind three children, aged eight, ten, and twelve. Ralph thought it was his duty to take the children in. Jane was too compliant to object, and so the kids moved in for the duration. Ralph's job required that he be gone a lot. Jane was left to rear the children mostly on her own. Nine years went by. Two of the kids left for college. Only a seventeen-year-old was left at home. In a few years, Jane thought she'd be home free. Not quite. Jane's body had grown lumpy, and Ralph's secretary, Sue, was a looker. Sue knew how to boost Ralph's ego. How could he help but fall in love? He and Sue knew their love was too real to be denied and too powerful to be resisted. Ralph divorced Jane to marry Sue. Ralph and Sue were happy. They found a new church that accepted them warmly. But Ralph needed one more stroke of acceptance, so he called Jane to ask her to forgive him and be glad for him that he was finally a happy man. "I want you to bless my new marriage," he said. Well, Jane told Ralph in very graphic terms where he could go. Forgive him? Throw away the only leverage she had—the strength of her hate? Her contempt was her power, her dignity, her self-esteem. It was unfair to ask her to forgive. The very least that louse deserved, in her mind, was a steady stream of scorn.[1]

Forgiveness is a funny thing. On one hand, forgiveness is a concept we all love because it is something we know we all need. But on the other hand, when we have been the one who has been wronged and wounded as deeply as Jane was, and we know we need to forgive, it becomes one of the most difficult things we ever are called to do. This becomes especially difficult when the wrong we suffered came at the hands of the person we love the most. At times like these, we wonder how we can forgive no matter how sorry they are. We all struggle with the whole idea of forgiveness, and I think there are a few key reasons why.

Many of us struggle with forgiveness because we think to forgive means we have to gloss over the seriousness of the offense. Not so. Forgiveness is not saying, "What you did was no big deal. It really

---

[1] Lewis Smedes, Forgive and Forget (San Francisco: Harper and Row, 1984), 128–129.

didn't hurt. Don't worry about it." The truth is if it's worth forgiving, it did hurt you. It did cause pain, and you don't need to minimize the seriousness of that offense because that's not a part of forgiveness. Forgiveness is saying, "Yes, it did hurt. Yes, it did cause me pain. But I'm going to let it go. I'm not going to hold it against you. I will relinquish my right to retaliate."

Many of us struggle with forgiveness because we believe forgiveness means we have to resume the relationship without change. Again this is not true. This is especially important to understand in a marriage relationship where trust has been broken. When adultery or abuse has occurred, you can forgive without necessarily jumping right back into the relationship. Your spouse may come to you and say, "I am so sorry. Will you forgive me?" At that point, you should offer forgiveness. It may take time but you must ultimately be willing to say I will forgive you because God has forgiven me and has commanded me in turn to forgive you." Forgiveness can be instant, but trust has to be rebuilt over time. So if they ask immediately, "Now that you have forgiven me, will you let me back in the house?" That's a different issue. You have every right to say, "Not now. We need to allow some time to transpire here. You need to get some counseling. You need to prove, over the course of time, that there is genuine repentance and change."

If you want to have a restored relationship with someone, first comes forgiveness. That's your part if you've been hurt. But for there to be an ongoing relationship, it takes genuine repentance and a rebuilding of trust, which takes time.

Many of us struggle with forgiveness because we have been taught to really forgive someone means you need to forget what happened. We've all heard the cliché forgive and forget. There's only one problem with that. You can't do it. It doesn't work. It's impossible for you to forget everything that has happened to you, and the more painful something was, the less likely it is that you are going really going to forget it. Forgiveness is not going to give you an instant case of amnesia.

If these things aren't what it means to forgive, you may ask, what is real forgiveness? I think the best definition I ever heard is that forgiveness is giving up your right to retaliate. Forgiveness is saying, "Yes it was a big deal. I can't just gloss it over. I can't go on right now as though nothing ever happened. That will take time. I can't just forget what transpired no matter how much I'd like to. But I choose not to retaliate, and I will not allow myself to be consumed by it because I will trust the Lord to deal with it." That's what forgiveness is.

Notice when I defined forgiveness, I said nothing about feelings. One thing you can not control is how you feel. You can not control your feelings. You can control your actions. If you feel sadness, pain, or even anger, none of those things are wrong. It's what you do with those things. If in my sadness, pain, and anger, I lash out in revenge, I'm wrong. If in my sadness, pain, or anger, I am bitter towards the person who has wronged me or I blame them for everything that's wrong in my life, I'm wrong. But if I feel sadness, pain, or anger and decide that even though I feel this way, I'm going to act differently; even though I feel this way, I'm going to do the right thing and not fight back, not retaliate, not be consumed by it, that is forgiveness. Forgiveness is based on actions and not on feelings.

But you may still wonder, how do I do this? How can I possibly forgive when the wounds are deep and the offenses are repeated? This is obviously something the apostle Peter struggled with. He came to Jesus one day and asked, "How many times must I forgive my brother who sins against me?" You know there is no doubt in my mind that this is not simply a hypothetical question. I believe Peter had a face and a name in mind. He's saying, Lord, this person has wronged me, and they have wounded me deeply and repeatedly. When can I stop forgiving and cut ties with this person? Then Peter asks Jesus, "Is seven times good enough?" Now where did Peter come up with this number seven? Well, the rabbis of Jesus day taught that you were to forgive a person who wronged you three times. After that, it was fair game to cut ties in the relationship and seek revenge. But don't forget, at this point Peter had been hanging around Jesus for awhile. He had gotten his arms around the truth that Jesus was much more forgiving and gracious than most people, and so he took what the rabbis taught, doubled it, and even added one for good measure! He thought that Jesus was going to be so proud of him for being willing to forgive seven times! Jesus responded, "No, seventy times seven."

What's Jesus saying? I believe Jesus is telling us that forgiveness is not a statistic; it's an attitude. If you're keeping score, it's not really forgiveness. Following this conversation with Peter, Jesus went on to tell a story, a parable, to drive home why Peter should be willing to forgive seventy times seven. The parable goes something like this:

A man owed a king a lot of money—10,000 talents. I have heard that estimated to be worth somewhere around twenty million dollars in today's economy. It was a big bill. He had no means to repay the king, so the king demanded he and his wife and kids be sold as repayment. But the slave fell on his face and said to the king, "Have patience, give me a little more time, and I'll repay you." The king had compassion on the man and cancelled the debt. He totally wiped the slate clean. I call that fairly generous, wouldn't you? If I forgive you $1, that's nothing really. If I really like you, I might forgive $5. If I really, really like you, maybe I would forgive $20. Beyond that, I don't know if I could like you that much. But this king canceled a debt of millions of dollars. He had deep compassion on the man and forgave the debt and let him go free. The man turned around and found someone who owed him a few denari (a few measly bucks) and demanded it be paid back immediately. The man fell on his face and said, "Please have patience. Give me some time. I promise to repay." Haven't we heard this before? Isn't that exactly what the servant said to the king? But the servant was unwilling to forgive or give more time to the man to pay that small amount of money back after the king had forgiven him such a huge debt. That doesn't make sense. When news of this got to the king, he was furious. He called the guy back in and said "What's the deal here? I forgave you this huge debt there was no way you could repay. Shouldn't you have had mercy on this guy?" And the king had the man thrown in jail until he could repay what he owed.

In this story, God is the king, and you and I are the debtors. So why should we forgive someone who has wounded us deeply and repeatedly? Why should we forgive seventy times seven?

The first and most obvious answer comes from this story. I should forgive because God has forgiven me of far greater offenses. Our motivation for forgiving others should begin by looking at how much God has forgiven us. In this story, the servant owes the king millions of dollars. Talk about back taxes! This guy was in debt up to his eyeballs. This was a huge amount of money, and there was absolutely no way he could ever repay this debt. Now in those days, there was no way to declare bankruptcy, so it was really simple how you dealt with such things. The normal procedure would be for the king to sell the servant's wife and kids as slaves and put the man in prison until he could repay the debt. But this guy begged the king for more time. "Don't throw me in jail right now. Don't sell my wife and kids. Give me a little more time." But the man knew in his heart there was no way he would ever be able to repay this debt. And the king knew there was no way he could repay the debt, and so he forgave the debt. He absorbed the loss and let the man off the hook with no strings attached. This king was magnificently generous! And the man seemed most grateful for the king's generosity. However, he quickly forgot what the king had done for him. He went out and found that man who owed him a few measly bucks and demanded payment immediately. This guy begged for a little more time, very much the way the servant had done with the king. But this man who had been forgiven the twenty million dollar debt could not find it in his heart to forgive this other man whose debt was miniscule compared to what he had been forgiven.

You know the reality is that if you have received Jesus as your Savior, God has forgiven you a mountain of sin debt that you could never possibly repay. It was totally a free gift of his grace. You didn't earn that forgiveness. You didn't deserve it. But God knew there was no possible way you could ever pay back the debt, and so He extended His forgiveness to you. And since we who have trusted Jesus as our Savior have been forgiven this mountain of sin debt we could never possibly repay, that should be motivation enough for us to forgive those who wrong us, even those closest to us whom we love, like our spouses and other family members, when they wound us deeply and repeatedly. You see, no matter how great the offense, it is still miniscule compared to your sins against God.

Maybe you're angry with your spouse because they lied to you intentionally, and you wonder how you could possibly forgive him/her. Let me ask you, have you ever lied? Has God forgiven you? Are you harboring resentment against your mate for some cruel words they spoke to you? Let me ask you, have you ever spoken cruel words about someone else? Has God forgiven you? Has your mate done some stupid thing that has caused you great grief and heartache and you wonder how you could possibly forgive him/her?

Here's how, and it's really the only way. Understand you have caused great grief and heartache to God because of your sin and disobedience. Realize he has willingly and repeatedly forgiven you. "Be kind and compassionate to one another, forgiving each other, just as in Christ, God forgave you," (Eph. 4:32). Notice how God forgave you. He forgave you simply because you are in Christ. Again, you're not forgiven because you earned it. You're not forgiven because you deserved it. You're not forgiven because you've promised never to sin again. You're forgiven because you are in Christ—you have trusted Him as your Savior. This is the starting point for genuine forgiveness. And our forgiveness of others ought to parallel this. We ought to forgive others, not because they deserve it, earn it, or promise to never do it again, but simply because Christ has forgiven us.

If you are still struggling to forgive someone, pause a minute and realize how much God has forgiven you. You will never have to suffer a greater debt to forgive anyone else than Jesus Christ suffered to forgive you. Not a chance. Remember how God has forgiven you. That's the only motivation that will allow us to forgive deep and repeated offenses. That's the primary reason we need to offer forgiveness.

There's a second reason we need to forgive, and it is also found in this story. We need to forgive because unforgiveness will destroy us. What did the king do when he found the servant he had forgiven so much had not been willing to forgive this measly debt this other man owed him? He had the man thrown into prison until he could pay the debt. Now if God is the king and we are the servants, an obvious question is, "Does this verse say that God's forgiveness of me is based on my willingness to forgive others? If I received Jesus Christ as Savior and God has forgiven me and I in turn fail to forgive someone else, is this saying that God is going to take my forgiveness and salvation away for failing to perform up to his expectation to forgive others?" Now at first glance, I can see why that question can arise in some people's minds. However, we need to look at the Bible as a whole and not get our thoughts from one individual passage of Scripture. The Bible is clear from beginning to end that salvation and forgiveness are never based on our performance. It's never a matter of what we do or don't do. We also know the Bible does not contradict itself. So is there another way to look at what Jesus is saying here? I believe there is. For this to make sense, you need to understand there are two types of forgiveness.

The first type of forgiveness is legal, or judicial, forgiveness. What I am talking about with legal, or judicial, forgiveness is having the debt for the crime that was committed, or in our case, the sins we have committed, cancelled. This is the forgiveness that takes place when we come to Jesus and receive him as our Savior. God legally forgives us, and our slate of sin is wiped clean in the courtroom of heaven. "For God was in Christ, reconciling the world to himself, no longer counting people's sins against them," (2 Cor. 5:19 NLT).

The moment that you trust Jesus Christ for salvation God will never count your sins against you again. Why? Because God's wrath over your sins was settled the moment you trusted Jesus for salvation and He paid the price for your sin in full. There is no double jeopardy in God's courtroom. He will never make you pay for your past, present, or future sin again. Why? Because they have already been paid for by Jesus. You have been legally forgiven.

The second type of forgiveness is relational forgiveness. That's what Jesus is talking about here. In this story, Jesus says if you aren't willing to forgive your brother who sins against you once you've been forgiven, God will treat you the way the king treated the servant. How did the king treat the servant? He threw him in jail until he could pay back what he owed the king. Again, is Jesus saying God will take our salvation away and throw us into the prison of hell if we don't forgive? No. That legal, or judicial, forgiveness was already settled at the cross. Then what is he saying? There's another way to look at this that makes more sense. What did the man owe the king? You might be inclined to answer twenty million dollars. But that's a wrong answer. He actually owed the king nothing. Why? Because the king had already forgiven that entire debt. He had already wiped the slate clean. That money was irrelevant now because the debt had been forgiven. So what did he owe the king? He owed the king a willingness to forgive the debts of others the way he had been forgiven. And when he refused to do that, he was thrown in jail until he could pay that debt. Until we are willing to forgive the debt of others against us, we will find ourselves locked up relationally with our Father. We may be forgiven, but we are not enjoying the real, dynamic relationship the Father wants us to experience. We will wonder, "Why are my prayers not being answered? Why does God seem so distant? Why does it seem like there's no blessing of God upon my life?" And the answer very well could be that it's because you are imprisoned by an unforgiving spirit. Not that you are again accountable for the debt of sin. That's already been forgiven because salvation is never a matter of performance. It's always and only a matter of grace. But you will find yourself imprisoned relationally if you have a spirit of unforgiveness.[2]

How well do you play this game of Sorry? Have you forgiven those loved ones who have wronged you? Here are two tests you might give yourself to find out if you have truly forgiven.

The Blame Test. If you have truly forgiven the person who wronged you, you won't continue to blame them for your unhappiness or the circumstances you find yourself facing in your life. If you are blaming them, you have not forgiven them.

The Bitterness Test. If you carry a mental balance sheet in your mind and every time the other person does something and you keep score, you haven't forgiven. Some of you know exactly what I'm talking about. You are living with and trying to forgive a mate who has made a major mistake in your marriage. And you are still holding it over their head. You're never going to be happy in that relationship again because you've made up your mind that everything they do from that day forward will never be enough to let them off the hook for what they have done to hurt you. If that is your attitude, let me assure you, you are the one who is killing your marriage by your bitterness. Bitterness will wreck your life. We can't afford to become bitter people. We need to learn to practice the art of forgiveness.

The game of Sorry is perhaps one of the most difficult games families play because sometimes we hurt those we love in ways that are deep. You may think you could never forgive, but you can. You can't ignore the hurt. You may or may not restore the relationship, depending on the seriousness of the offense, but you can forgive. You can give up your right to retaliate by remembering how much God has forgiven you and refusing to be imprisoned by unforgiveness.

---

[2] Tony Evans, God's Pardon through Prayer, audiotape (Dallas: The Urban Alternative).

Chapter 7

. . . .

Hungry, Hungry Hippos

When Two Become Three or More

You may wonder what the game Hungry, Hungry Hippos, where you have to gobble up the marbles as fast as you can into the mouth of the hippos, has to do with Games Families Play. If you are asking that question, you haven't had kids! Nothing changes our lives faster than when these hungry, demanding children arrive in our homes, does it? Which of the following statements are true?

- Children are a wonderful addition to a marriage.
- Children put a great deal of stress upon a marriage.

Obviously, both of these statements are true. Children are a wonderful addition to the life of a couple. The Bible says in Psalm 127:3, "Children are a gift from the Lord; they are a reward from Him," (NLT). One of the greatest joys that Tricia and I had was when we welcomed each of our five children into our family. God has blessed us with four sons, who were born to us biologically, and a daughter, who was born in our hearts through adoption. Every one of them brings something different to our family, and we can't imagine our lives without them.

It is also true that children put a great deal of stress upon a marriage. When a mother's body begins to change during pregnancy and she's tired or sick all the time, there is stress. Making sure the house is prepared and the baby's room properly decorated for the new arrival can create panic attacks. Pacing back and forth as the contractions start and stop and wondering when will it happen for real can raise tensions. When the baby arrives and takes over the home with his or her middle-of-the-night feedings and sleepless nights, fatigue can set in as both mom and dad are exhausted and may even argue over who's turn it is to get up with the baby this time. There's constant care to be given, diapers to be changed, new restrictions on your freedom, and all of these things and much more can create a great deal of stress. That's just in the early years!

As children get older, there is discipline to be given out and sometimes mom and dad don't always agree on when and how this discipline should occur. There are schedules to keep that include extracurricular activities like ball practices, recitals, and school events, and all these things add to the pressure we already had in our lives and marriages before children came along.

And then we face the teenage years, with kids entering the world of driving and dating and holding down jobs etc. Need I say more? There is stress! When children enter into our lives, there is no way of understating the stress that puts upon a relationship and the stress we put upon ourselves to effectively handle this new responsibility. There is no way we can possibly ever anticipate all the changes parenthood brings. But probably the biggest change is in our marriage. So how do we navigate the changes that having children bring into marriage and ensure both a solid marriage and family?

Make sure your relationship with your spouse takes precedence over your relationship with your children. This is important. Remember that verse from Genesis 2:24? "For this reason a man will leave his father and mother and be united to his wife, and they will become one flesh." When a man and woman are joined together as husband and wife, that relationship is to take priority over every other relationship in their lives, including their relationships with parents and, when the time comes, with their children. There is no doubt that as parents, the responsibility of raising children has to be one of the top priorities in our lives. It is true that I have seen many couples who do not place this high enough on the list of priorities. But I have also seen many couples who go to the other extreme and make children the center of the home. Children are a great blessing to a marriage, but they are not to be the focal point of it. Let me put it this way, if you have a child-centered home, it gives that child the idea that they are the center of the universe—that everything in life is all about them. The marriage relationship was created by God to be the foundation of a healthy home, and if our focus on our children takes priority over our mate, that foundation will crumble.

This is a great danger we have to be careful to avoid. Don't allow yourself to become so obsessed with your children that you put that most important relationship, your marriage, in jeopardy. It is so easy for us to think, This is just a season of life. For now, we will build our lives upon our children, and later we will prioritize our marriage once again. I have seen many couples who fall into this trap, only to one day wake up and find the children are gone and their relationship has deteriorated to a point where they don't even know each other anymore. Thus, there is no longer an obvious reason to remain together because they have built their home for the last twenty years on the wrong foundation, the foundation of child-rearing instead of the foundation of their relationship as husband as wife. That's why divorce rates soar among empty nesters.

God never intended for it to be that way. He gave us children as a great blessing to our marriages, but He never intended for children to be the focus of that relationship. Please understand that the most important relationship in any family, the foundation, the glue that holds the family together, is the relationship between husband and wife. You do your children a great disservice when you prioritize your relationship with them over your relationship with your mate. Why? Because children need security. And much of that security comes from a stable home where mom and dad love each other. So make your relationship as husband and wife the number one relationship in your home. Someday your children will grow up and leave home—at least you hope they will! If you have built your life around them, what will happen then?

Make sure mom and dad present a unified front to your children. It is vital for children to know early on that they can't pit mom against dad or vice versa. My kids have tried this several times. When Mom says, "No," they run to me. Or when I say, "No," they run to Mom. They found out quickly this wasn't going to work. If children think they can get away with it, they will learn to make a deal with one parent and run an end around the other parent. So it's vital for parents to present a unified front and support one another and not allow this to happen.

When a child wants to spend the night at someone's house or goes somewhere with friends or buys something special or desires some other privilege, mom and dad need to learn to say, "Let me ask your mom, or let me ask your dad, and get back with you." Then they should consult in private and come up with an answer. When parents hash it out in private and then present a unified front to the children with their answer, it keeps one parent from looking like the bad guy for saying no when the other parent has already let the child know if it were up to them they would say yes.

This is also important when it comes to the area of discipline. It is another area where kids will quickly pick up if mom and dad are not together. The Bible tells us if we really love our children we will discipline them. "If you refuse to discipline your children, it proves you don't love them; if you love your children, you will be prompt to discipline them," (Prov. 13:24 NLT). It can't get any clearer than that. Yet discipline is one of those areas many parents struggle with. Let me share some suggestions for discipline.

1. Discipline consistently. Many parents make a mistake here. If we aren't consistent in our approach to discipline, children quickly discover the rules don't always apply, but rather they depend upon circumstances such as what kind of mood mom and dad happen to be in. If they find they can get away with anything when you're in a good mood but when you're in a grumpy mood they had better watch out, this will create problems for them because they won't really understand what the appropriate behavioral boundaries are. So be consistent. The goal of discipline is to teach children the appropriate boundaries, and these boundaries should not shift.

2. Discipline calmly. Discipline should not be an opportunity for us to take our frustrations out on our kids. I have to confess there are times when I have been guilty of this. I know I have reacted out of anger and yelled at my kids simply because I was frustrated, not because they were being bad. How foolish I look and feel when I do that. How can you know when you are reacting in anger and not disciplining in love? Look at your child's reaction. If they look afraid, then you probably are disciplining out of anger. "Don't make your children angry by the way you treat them. Rather, bring them up with the discipline and instruction approved by the Lord," (Eph. 6:4 NLT).

3. Discipline correctively. There is a difference between discipline and punishment. Punishment is meant to inflict penalty because of something you did that was wrong. Discipline on the other hand is meant as a correction for future behavior. In discipline, you are letting them know you did not approve of some past behavior and you are holding them accountable for that behavior. But more importantly, you don't want the child to do this again in the future. Our desire should be to help our children establish appropriate boundaries in their life where we eventually don't have to apply

nearly as much discipline. So when you discipline your children for inappropriate behavior, take time to talk to them about why it is inappropriate and how they can make changes the next time. Don't simply penalize inappropriate behavior; share with them the appropriate behavior for the future. The motivation behind discipline is love. It is saying to our kids, "I want you to make it in this world, and I love you enough to apply discipline where necessary to correct your behavior."

4. Discipline creatively. Our five children are all different. Some respond well to scolding and quickly obey. Some clam up when scolded and withdraw. When disciplining, you have to be creative. We have one child who is just mortified if you scold him verbally. We have another child who acts like he could care less. We have one who goes to his room and is quickly sorry for what he has done. We have another who acts like being alone in his room is really not that big of a deal. Look for what works with your child. Don't assume you can treat them all the same.

5. Discipline conservatively. Your discipline will be much more effective and corrective when you don't discipline your children for every little thing they do. "Fathers, don't scold your children so much that they become discouraged and quit trying," (Col. 3:21 TLB). So mom and dad should make sure they are on the same page when it comes to discipline. Don't allow your children to play divide and conquer.

Make sure you take time to develop a relationship with your children. While your marriage has to be the number one relationship in your family, don't go to the other extreme and shut your kids out. Don't treat them as a nuisance in your life.

Dad, you are the most important man in the life of your children. Mom, you are the most important woman. Your kids desperately need you, and what they need from you more than anything is a relationship. Having a close, loving relationship with your children is vital to being a successful parent. In fact, I would go so far as to say that the most important gift you can give your kids is the gift of a loving relationship. You might say, "Wait a minute! That sounds sacrilegious. I thought teaching my kids the truth about a relationship with Jesus was the most important gift I could give my children." But I would suggest to you that this is even more important. If you do not first of all have a relationship with your kids, they will probably reject your Jesus. Please understand that a relationship with your kids is no guarantee that you will be successful as a parent. They could still grow up to rebel against your authority and reject your Jesus. On the other hand, if you don't have a relationship with them, I can almost guarantee you that you will fail as a parent. A solid relationship with our kids at least gives us a fighting chance at success.

You need to understand that while your kids will not admit it, they are crying out for a relationship with you more than anyone else on the face of the earth. Studies indicate that the strongest deterrent against kids having problems with drugs, alcohol, violence, or teenage pregnancy is a close relationship with their parents. Research among twelve- to fourteen-year- olds indicates that they are three times more likely to commit suicide if there is no close relationship with mom and dad. Research among fifteen- to sixteen-year-olds indicates that they are four times more likely to commit suicide if there is no close relationship with mom and dad, and seventeen- to nineteen-year-olds are twice as likely to commit suicide if there is no close relationship with mom and dad. Parents, our kids desperately need a relationship with us more than anyone.[1]

Pop singer Michael Jackson spoke at Oxford a few years ago, and in the middle of his speech, he began to weep, talking about his dad. He told about how his dad was a great manager and promoter, but then he said this, "What I really wanted was a dad. I wanted a father

---

[1] Quoted by Josh McDowell, Extreme Service: Lover, Mentor, Leader, audiotape (Auburn Hills: Promise Keepers, 2001)

who showed me love. And my father never did that. He never said I love you while looking me straight in the eye; he never played a game with me. He never gave me a piggyback ride; he never threw a pillow at me, or a water balloon. But I remember once when I was about four years old, there was this carnival, and he picked me up and put me on a pony. It was a tiny gesture, probably something he forgot five minutes later. But because of that moment, I have a special place in my heart for him."[2] What was he saying? He was saying what I wanted more than anything else was a relationship with the most important man in my life. If you want to be a successful parent, don't miss out on developing a relationship with your kids.

Make sure you don't try to parent alone. If you try to parent in your own power, you are going to fail. It takes God's love. Human love wears out. There is a limit to how much you can handle. There are days and nights when you don't have any more to give and you know it. There are times when you are so worn out that you want to tell your kids to go take care of themselves. What you need more than anything else is God's strength. God is love. And it's only when we experience His love in our lives and have a personal relationship with Him that we can, in turn, really learn to love others. Don't try to do it on your own! You need God's help.

If you will make sure you do these things, you can successfully navigate this tough journey called parenting.

---

[2] Ibid

Chapter

8

$\bullet \bullet$

Pictionary

What Does the Picture of a Healthy Family Look Like?

One Saturday, we worked all morning to get our five kids cleaned up and ready to go a portrait studio to have our family picture taken. This took a whole lot of effort and we found ourselves running late. When we finally arrived, the photographer seemed rushed and preoccupied. The end result was that we didn't like any of the pictures. After all that work, we ended up going home without buying anything! Then my wife called another studio and informed us that the next Saturday we were going to turn around and do the whole thing all over again!

It's hard to get a good family picture isn't it? With the family unit in such desperate condition in America today, people have a difficult time knowing what the picture of a healthy family looks like. We have experienced escalating numbers in . . . divorce rates . . . kids who spend some weekends at mom's house and some weekends at dad's house . . . spousal abuse . . . teenage suicides . . . births out of wedlock. The numbers have not been good for the American family. This has caused many people to ask if the idea of a family unit is obsolete. Is it irrelevant? Should we forget the whole idea of the family?

I don't believe the family is finished. It's fragmented. We may not recognize it if we saw it. What does a healthy family look like? In every community there are four places you will find that are necessary for a well-functioning community. I believe that these four places give us huge insight into what a healthy family ought to look like.

A Hospital

The first picture is that of a hospital. What's a hospital for? Obviously, it's a place to go when you are injured or sick and in need of healing. Every day each family member leaves home and goes out into a cruel and uncaring world. Moms and dads go to work and often experience a cut-throat environment that is full of competition where people could care less about their personal lives. They're only concerned about the bottom line. Children go to school and rub shoulders all day with other children who can be undoubtedly cruel and insensitive. Then at the end of the day, one by one, we arrive home bruised, bleeding, sometimes even emotionally sick and in need of some medical attention to restore us to health. Where do we get that emotional medical treatment we so desperately need? I believe God intended for it to be found within our families. A healthy family is a place where, day in and day out, healing can happen. It is a place where wounds can be bandaged and we can feel reenergized and revitalized, so we can go out and face a rough, tough world for another day. The medicine that will heal these emotional wounds that are inflicted from the world around us is unconditional love. You don't get that anywhere else in the world. When you go out into the world you hear things like, "I'll love you if . . . ," or "I'll love you when . . . ," or "I'll love you because . . . ." But in the home, we should hear and experience an atmosphere that simply says, "I love you—period." "I love you just because you are you." And there is incredible healing for wounded hearts when that type of love exists in the home.

Every day, each member of the family needs to come home to this healing atmosphere of unconditional love. But the question is, if every member of the family needs this same medical attention at the end of the day, who's going to be the doctor? Who's going to provide the medical attention necessary to bring us back to health? Well, I believe the Bible is very clear. Everyone in the family has the responsibility of being both doctor and patient at the family hospital.

In Ephesians 5:25, we read, "Husbands, love your wives, just as Christ loved the church and gave himself up for her." So men, husbands, and fathers, it starts with you. You have to be the first one to provide this unconditional love for your wife. You will set the tone for whether or not the healing of unconditional love happens in your home.

But wives and moms, that doesn't let you off the hook. Titus 2:4 says, "Train the younger women to love their husbands." You are called, in turn, to provide medical attention for your husband's wounds with your unconditional love. You also have to be the doctor and attend to the needs of your husband.

And then the Bible instructs parents together to love their children. So moms and dads, you have the responsibility to put on the doctor's jackets and bandage the wounds your children come home with and heal them with your unconditional love. Children need this badly, and if they don't get this kind of love at home, they will look for it somewhere else, often in places we would never want them to go.

Children have a responsibility too. "Children, obey your parents in the Lord, for this is right. 'Honor your father and mother'—which is the first commandment with a promise," (Eph. 6:1–2)—And as children obey and honor in this way, in a very real sense, they too provide strength and healing to their parents.

An unconditional, life-giving love is given and received in a healthy family. But the sad truth is that many homes instead of being a hospital where healing takes place through unconditional love become a place where more wounds are inflicted. Not so with a healthy family. Healthy families vow to never abuse, shame, control, or intimidate each other. Abuse in the family is, in the opinion of many, the most devastating thing anyone can go through. The most deeply wounded people on our planet today are those who have looked to family members for love and nurturing and affirmation and instead have received abuse of some kind that devastates their lives. You see, when a child is longing for emotional support from mom and dad and instead receives emotional abuse, or when a child is yearning for tender words and instead gets verbally abused, or when a child is longing for a reaffirming physical touch and instead receives physical abuse, it can wound their hearts in ways that they never recover from the rest of their lives. They may find themselves struggling with ever giving or receiving unconditional love as long as they live.

If that in any way describes your home, you need to know that it is not normal. Maybe it's the way things were in the family you grew up in and you never knew any different, but I want to assure you, you can and must break that pattern of abuse. Healthy families vow to never abuse each other in any way. It's a tragedy when, rather than being a place where hearts are healed with unconditional love, a home becomes a place where hearts are wounded, sometimes to never be healthy again.[1]

A School

A second picture of a healthy family is that of a school house. Our kids spend twelve years, or more, in school learning reading, writing, and arithmetic, but in the family school they spend about eighteen years learning things that prepare them for life. You learn basic life skills in the family school house that you probably won't, and really shouldn't, get anywhere else.

The home is a school house and, like it or not, your values are going to be taught to your children. Intentionally or unintentionally your children are going to get a sense of where your true values lie.

---

[1] Adapted from Bill Hybels, The Home as a Filling Station, audiotape (Chicago: Seeds Tape Ministry).

What are some areas we need to be sure to train our children in? I believe there are four significant values our children should never leave home without.

Train your children in the value of work.

Col. 3:23 says, "Whatever you do, work at it with all your heart, as working for the Lord, not for men." We need to teach our children to work hard and do their best at whatever they do simply because of who they work for. And it is our responsibility as parents to instill this value of work in them. I grew up in a home where we had daily chores. We weren't allowed to sit back and watch Mom and Dad do it all. I was taught the value of work. Young people in the Bible often had chores to do. David looked after his father's sheep. Miriam looked after her brother Moses. Samuel assisted Eli in the temple.

John Rosemond in his book A Family of Value talks about how the value of work is not being taught to today's generation of children as consistently as it used to be. "Yesterday's parents saw to it that by age four, children had been inducted into full, contributory participation in their families. They accomplished this by assigning their children chores. Not just occasional chores here or there, mind you, but routines of chores that consumed blocks of time each and every day. Shortly after his or her third birthday (if not before), a child was given a 'job description' concerning his or her role in the family. Initially, this job description was limited to helping older members of the family carry out their chores. Once the child had learned a job, it was transferred to him. In relatively short order, the child was 'pulling his weight.' As he gained weight, he pulled even more weight until he had learned enough to be able to take over other family members jobs at a moments notice."[2]

---

[2] John Rosemond, A Family of Value (Kansas City, MO: Andrews and McNeel, 1995), 173–174.

We try to practice this in our home. Our children have chores and are expected to do them right. If they do not, they must go back and redo them. They don't like to do this. They will fight against it. And sometimes the easy way out is for Mom and Dad to say, "It's not worth the hassle. I'll do it myself." But don't let that happen. The value of work is a necessary value for children to learn in the home school house. Don't neglect this important area.

The reasons to train children in the value of work are many and far-reaching.

1. Participation in family work confirms the child as a valued member of the family. The more responsibility the child accepts, the more status he or she will have in the eyes of his or her parents and siblings.

2. The child learns the principle of give and take. Children need to understand that you have to give something to get something out of life.

3. Chores enhance the value of the family to the child. Chores are a means of bonding the child to the values that enhance and enrich the family.[3]

Don't miss teaching this important value to your children. Teach them the value of being contributing members of the family, and start at a young age.

Train your children in the value of relationships. Life is a series of relationships. We need to teach our children the value of building, nurturing, and rebuilding relationships. We learn to relate to others in the home. Good or bad, right or wrong, to a great degree your happiness and success in life depends upon your ability to relate to other people. And you learn that at home. We need to help our children develop relational skills. They need to know that relationships can and often do break down. When that happens, they need to learn

---

[3] Ibid.

to rebuild relationships through communication and reconciliation. Somehow we've got to get past the popular idea in our society that relationships are disposable, that when something goes wrong at home or work or church we can walk away. We need to teach our children that when relationships break down, we can't simply give up and walk away, but rather that relationships are so valuable; they are worth the hard work it takes to mend and resolve problems.

Isn't that what Jesus taught about relationships? If your brother has something against you, don't ignore the situation, don't hold a grudge, don't slam the door and walk away, but rather go to your brother and reconcile the situation. Parents, if you allow your children to constantly pout and walk away instead of working on resolving relationships, what will happen later in their life when the stakes are even higher? Will they simply walk away from their marriage or job or any other area in which they have to deal with people?

One of the most important values we can impart to family members is to work on relationships, nurture them, and reconcile them to the best of our ability when they get broken. It takes a lot of training but it's worth the effort.

Train your children about the value of character. The it-doesn't-matter-how-you-succeed-as-long-as-you-succeed principle seems to be taught in many homes today. And in the process character is often shoved aside. Children need to learn it does matter how you succeed. Children today are being challenged athletically, academically, and artistically at earlier and earlier ages, and the message is coming across to many young people that you need to do what it takes to win no matter what the cost. Who's reminding our children that it does matter how you play the game? It has to happen in the home. We ought to take very seriously the responsibility to teach our children the value of character.

Train your children about the value of money. Children want everything, or so it seems. We seldom go to Wal-Mart or a toy store without our kids pointing out everything in sight that they want. I find it's sometimes hard to say no, and because it's hard to say no, many parents easily say yes and give kids almost everything they want. Consequently, too many children grow up with little appreciation for the value of money. They grow up knowing money buys things that they like, but often they don't learn about the value of money.

They need to learn from mom and dad about handling money properly. In our home we give our children an allowance. Out of it is a certain amount that is their tithe to the Lord, a certain amount that is to go into savings, and then the rest is theirs to use for things they want. If they want something that is more than what they have left, they are encouraged to save for it. Teach your children the value of money.[4]

A Playground

A third picture of a healthy family is that of a playground. Healthy families play together. They have fun together. Now I'm not saying that mom needs to crack jokes all the time or dad needs to dress up like a clown and entertain the kids, but I am saying that a home should be a place where fun and laughter is a natural part of the atmosphere. Sometimes we get so busy with life we tend to forget to make time for fun. But a family ought to be a place to kick back, relax, and have fun. The Bible says in Psalm 127, "Children are a gift from God." As I listen to a lot of parents, I quickly get the impression that they're enduring their kids, not enjoying them. But don't forget they are a gift, and gifts are meant to be enjoyed, not just endured. Our children bring much laughter to our lives.

---

[4] Adapted from Bill Hybels, The Home as a Training Center, audiotape (Chicago: Seeds Tape Ministry).

Our teenage son, Michael, is developing a quick-witted sense of humor. The other day in his class at church they were talking about the woman at the well who been married five times and was now living with a man who wasn't her husband. The teacher asked, "What do you think this woman needed?" To which my son responded with deep spiritual maturity instilled by his father, "A lawyer!"

Our second oldest son, David, has always been one to do what he can to try to make us laugh. Even when he was preschool age, if he got a laugh out of something, he'd continue to do it time and again. We have a number of different pictures of him doing funny things like wearing underwear on his head, wearing one of my ties wrapped around his neck, wearing his grandpa's cowboy boots that swallowed up the entire lower half of his body, standing in only a diaper and pointing a squirt gun at us, and other such interesting things!

Our youngest sons, Adam and Joshua, are only a year apart and act like twins. They play together constantly, and one of the things they love to play is dress up. We gave them Batman and Spiderman outfits for Christmas this year, and we chuckle as they run around battling each other in their superhero garb.

We laugh almost daily at our youngest daughter, Rachel. She is such an outgoing little girl. She is only three but not afraid to talk to anyone or to say anything that might happen to be on her mind. On a recent flight back to our parents' house in Indiana, Rachel sat between Tricia and a young man, who obviously wanted to sleep the entire flight. Rachel had tons of energy and couldn't understand why. She poked at him every few minutes and asked Tricia, "Mommy, why is that guy sleeping?" Fortunately, he would open his eyes, smile at her, and then close his eyes again! With five kids, there is never a dull moment.

There are times parenting can be tough. But don't forget your kids are not going to be with you forever. Enjoy them while you can. Someday they will grow up. You may think that things will be a whole lot different. Someday you will clean the house and it will stay that way for more than five minutes. Someday you won't trip over toys every time you walk through the family room. Someday the refrigerator won't be filled with five gallons of milk. Someday there won't be Happy Meal toys left all over the car. Someday you will actually be able to use the bathroom by yourself! In fact, someday the entire house will be quiet and clean and filled with memories and lonely and we won't like it. When that happens, we will wonder where it all went. How did all those days go by so quickly?

We don't have forever. Make your home a fun place. Enjoy your kids. If your home isn't fun when your kids are growing up, don't be surprised if they don't come back as often as you'd like when they are grown. Healthy families have fun.

A Church

The last picture of a healthy family is that of a church—a place where spiritual training takes place. One of the reasons God established the family is so young people would grow up to know and love Him. "Has not the Lord made them one? In flesh and spirit they are his. And why one? Because he was seeking godly offspring," (Mal. 2:15). The moment you decided to have children, you took on a whole lot of responsibilities, and one of those responsibilities is to teach spiritual things to your children. I have heard it said many times that Christianity is always one generation away from extinction. As parents, we need to take seriously the responsibility to train our children to know and love the Lord.

Clear back in the Old Testament Moses instructed the Israelites about the seriousness of passing their faith from one generation to the next. "And you must think constantly about these commandments I am giving you today. You must teach them to your children and talk about them when you are at home or out for a walk; at bedtime and the first thing in the morning. Tie them on your finger, wear them on your forehead, and write them on the doorposts of your house!"

(Deut. 6:6–9 TLB). Moses recognized the passing on of the faith was not a one-time event like a baptism. It is a daily discipline. He's saying don't allow yourselves to become complacent and automatically assume that your children are going to grow up to know and worship your God. You've got to be intentional about it.

There are four key words in those verses. The first one is you. You have the responsibility to train your children in spiritual things. You are the real youth pastors. The youth ministry programs at your church or the Christian school your kids may attend are there to supplement your efforts at youth ministry, not to provide all of the training. You are the ones who have the primary responsibility. I heard someone say one time that what some parents want is a Christian laundry service. You drop the kids off at church and say, "Here's my kid. Educate him, baptize him, sanctify him, and I'll pick him up when he's eighteen! But it's not primarily the church's job to teach spiritual things to your children; it's primarily your job. Don't simply put this responsibility off on someone else.

When our children were young, we regularly read them Bible stories, helped them memorize Bible verses, and prayed with them. As they have gotten older, we require them to do their own personal devotions and prayer time in the mornings before school, and we occasionally do family devotions when we are all together at the dinner table. We talk about the things of God and how we can live those things out in our lives.

You can't simply pass the job of youth ministry off to the church. Children will learn the priority of Jesus Christ in your life by your attitude toward church. I grew up in a preacher's home, and I was taught at an early age that Jesus was the number one priority of our lives and that being in church to learn about Him and worship Him was never an optional part of our schedule. Every time the church doors were opened, I never asked, "Are we going?" I knew better. I simply asked, "What time are we leaving?" There were Sundays that

I would rather have slept in or stayed home Sunday night to watch the end of a ball game, but it didn't happen.

I have heard parents say, "I'm not going to make my kids go to church. I don't want to force my religion down their throat. I don't want to turn them off, you know." While I'm sure the intentions of those parents are noble, that line of reasoning doesn't make a whole lot of sense, does it? How often do we use that line of reasoning in other areas when it comes to raising our kids? We force them to do many things they don't want to do simply because we know it is best for them. We force them to take showers, even when they believe cleanliness is about as far from godliness as you could possibly get. We force them to a take medicine the doctor has said is necessary whether they like the taste or not. We force them to go to school no matter what excuse they come up with. Here's the bottom line; if we make them go to school and not to church, they will quickly get the idea that learning about God is optional, while the three Rs are priority stuff.

I will never forget the time I made the all-star team in Little League baseball. I was never more excited about anything in my life. Until the schedule came out and I realized the games conflicted with our church schedule. That meant I wasn't going to be able to play on the team. I begged and pleaded with my parents to let me miss church for this one thing. It didn't work. I cried and threw temper tantrums to no avail. Some of you might read that and say, "Oh you poor kid. How could your parents do that to you?" But today I am glad I had parents who knew they had to take seriously this responsibility that God had given to them. They communicated to me that He was number one in their life and in our family.

The second key word is must. You must constantly teach these things to your children. Moses isn't saying you can if you have the time, but it's okay to ignore teaching spiritual things to your children if you're too busy. He says you must do it.

The third key word is teach. What must you do? Teach your children the things of God. Parents, you are teaching all the time whether you realize it or not. If your children are around you, you're teaching them. They're watching every move you make. They're seeing how you live your life. When you sleep in on Sunday and skip church because you're tired but you go to work day after day under the same conditions, you've taught them where your real priorities lie. When you laugh at crude or profane things that come across your television screen for entertainment, you've taught them about holiness. When you go to the liquor closet or medicine cabinet to calm your nerves, you've taught them where to put their trust. You're teaching constantly whether you realize it or not. Are you teaching the right things?

The fourth key word is commandments. What must you teach? These commandments, these instructions, from God that I'm giving you. I've heard people say, "I'm not going to impose my spiritual values on my kids. When it comes to God, I'm going to let them decide for themselves." That doesn't make any sense. What they're basically saying is God is an optional part of life that you have to decide on for yourself. But he's not an option. He is the true and living God, and our kids must learn that from us. Moses says you must do this. You're hurting your kids if you're teaching them God is an option. Moses said if you're going to teach these things to your children, you make it part of your family life all the time. Talk about the things of God when you're at home, out for a walk, first thing in the morning, and last thing in the evening. You must demonstrate this constantly and consistently. Your faith should not be reserved for church only. It ought to be part of your every day activities as well.

Simple things are important. Things like reading Bible stories to children when they are younger and teaching them to do daily devotions as they get older. Things like praying together at meal times and bed times. Things like intentional conversations that deal with Christian morals and values. All these things can have a huge impact upon young lives. Your home has to be a church, where your children are intentionally taught the things of God.

How healthy is your family? Is your family a hospital where healing takes place, or are deeper wounds inflicted there? Is your family a school where your children are taught life lessons? What about a playground—do you have fun together or simply tolerate one another? What about a church? You must teach the things of God to your children. It is primarily your responsibility.

These are some of the Games Families Play. The stakes are high. These are real life games at which we can't afford to lose. We have to play to win. Our spouses need us to play to win. Our children need us to play to win. A watching world, who needs to see an example of a Christ-like family, needs us to play to win. Let's do all we can to follow God's game plan, play hard, and play to win!

To order additional copies of

GAMES
FAMILIES PLAY

Have your credit card ready and call:

1-877-421-READ (7323)

or please visit our web site at
www.pleasantword.com

Also available at:
www.amazon.com
and
www.barnesandnoble.com

Printed in the United States
26356LVS00006B/157-171